Cinematography

FilmCraft

Cinematography

Mike Goodridge
& Tim Grierson

AMSTERDAM • BOSTON • HEIDELBERG • LONDON
NEW YORK • OXFORD • PARIS • SAN DIEGO
SAN FRANCISCO • SINGAPORE • SYDNEY • TOKYO
Focal Press is an imprint of Elsevier

Focal Press

ELSEVIER

Focal Press is an imprint of Elsevier Inc.
225 Wyman Street, Waltham
MA 02451, USA

This book was conceived, designed, and produced by
Ilex Press Limited, 210 High Street, Lewes, BN7 2NS, UK

Publisher: Alastair Campbell
Creative Director: Peter Bridgewater
Associate Publisher: Adam Juniper
Managing Editors: Natalia Price-Cabrera and Zara Larcombe
Editor: Tara Gallagher
Art Director: James Hollywell

In-house designer: Kate Haynes
Design: Grade Design

Color Origination: Ivy Press Reprographics

Library of Congress Control Number:
A catalog record for this book is available from the Library
of Congress.

Special thanks to Caroline Bailey, Dave Kent, Darren Thomas,
Phil Moad, and Cheryl Thomas at The Kobal Collection, for all of
their effort and support.

Every effort has been made to acknowledge pictures.
However, the publisher apologizes if there are any unintentional
omissions.

ISBN: 978-0-240-81862-7
For information on all Focal Press publications visit our
website at:
www.focalpress.com

Printed and bound in China

10 9 8 7 6 5 4 3 2 1

Table of Contents

Introduction

The peculiar alchemy that makes up a great film is rarely achieved—little wonder, considering the demands on the team of people who must come together to support a common vision. It starts with the screenplay and over time crystallizes into another form through the efforts of the producer and director, actors, production and costume designers, cinematographer, editor, composer, and scores of others in each department. And, film being the most expensive art form to realize, the team is working under pressures of time and finance that can often harm—although sometimes enhance—the finished work.

There is no formula for making a film. Like a building, it is constructed from the ground up each time, using the basic blueprint of script and director. Knowledge and experience are key, but beyond that a film requires that special, indefinable vision that all great artists possess. For that reason, the FilmCraft project can never be a simple "how to" guide to the crafts; each subject will illustrate his or her process, but what makes them unique cannot be learned or replicated.

The cinematographer—or director of photography—is often the key conduit for all the other craftspeople on a film set. Through the cinematographer's lens, all performance, direction, and design must pass, and the cinematographer's own choices in cameras, lighting, and movement can inform and further the story in both obvious and subtle ways.

In the early days of cinema, the director also operated the camera; lighting was provided by direct sunlight or sunlight diffused by the glass ceilings of early studios. But by the turn of the century, as filmmaking became more sophisticated and films began to consist of multiple shots and locations, a breed of specialist camera operators emerged. Artificial lighting on sound stages was added to the mix, beginning an era of creative lighting that could change the mood and look of a film entirely. The use of different lenses, the introduction of color, and ongoing technical innovations throughout the twentieth century gave rise to an explosion of creative solutions and interpretations on the part of filmmakers who repeatedly defied convention to establish particular looks and moods.

The cinematographer is no longer merely the camera operator, but leads a team of people that often includes an operator, a focus puller, loader, grip and gaffer (see Glossary, page 188). The best cinematographers take the job of being a leader very seriously. "As a Director of Photography, I direct everything that has to do with photography," **Eternal Sunshine of the Spotless Mind** DP Ellen Kuras says. "Yet, I don't simply see myself as a cinematographer. I'm very embracing and caring of the crew and everything that goes on around me. That means the art department, the wardrobe, everything. Those people are under my wing, and I'm gonna take care of them. It's my responsibility."

Working with the director, the cinematographer establishes the composition of a scene, the way it is lit, the movement of the camera in relation to the actors or location, and can often have a say, alongside the director and designers, on which colors should be used. "Not all directors are visual," cinematographer Ed Lachman told us. "So you have to find your footing with the director for how you create that language, because for me the language of cinema is images. The images are the subtext for the psychological world that you create for the characters."

Budget levels are another factor. Hong Kong-based Christopher Doyle, for example, has worked on largely non-US films, mostly not in English, with budgets that are often a fraction of what would be devoted to a Hollywood studio blockbuster. Doyle says that part of his art consists of working out the most creative solution within the confines of budget and location.

It is often the most ostentatiously grand imagery that gets official recognition from the Academy of Motion Picture Arts and Sciences. Only when the images captured are extraordinary and the colors breathtaking do some viewers believe they are watching the work of a great DP. In the first decade of this century Oscars have gone, as is traditional, to large spectacles, period pieces and stories that encompass beautiful widescreen vistas or seascapes. And while epic films like **The Lord of the Rings**, **Master and Commander**, **The Aviator**, and **Avatar** require a huge amount of planning and preparation to capture those shots, cinematographers will tell you that the most challenging—and perhaps, therefore, the "best"—work is done when operating in a tiny apartment or alleyway. But maybe that's the point of good cinematography: You can't notice it. It influences, guides, and moves you on a subconscious level.

As the following 16 interviews will demonstrate, no two DPs are alike and all are fascinating, sometimes eccentric personalities with strong opinions and ideas. Take Vittorio Storaro, one of the living legends in the field. His credits speak for themselves. **The Conformist**, **Last Tango in Paris**, **Apocalypse Now**, **Reds**, **The Last Emperor**, and **Dick Tracy** are just a few of them. Storaro has developed a rich philosophy about lighting and color which relates to art, literature, and philosophy through the ages. Colors have specific meanings in the work of Storaro and lighting is designed to tell a story. He has written three books on his theories.

Others prefer to rely on spontaneity and instinct, working without lighting design plans or color schemes and implanting impromptu meaning into light and color while on set. Some resent storyboards as limiting their creativity; others prefer not to work with directors who insist on dictating all the cinematography decisions. Some like to come to the first meeting with the director full of ideas, some want to talk to the director without any preconceived notions. But none of them want to be pigeonholed, either to a particular type of film or shooting style. Take Rodrigo Prieto, who has worked extensively with director Alejandro González Iñárritu. Although he brilliantly incorporates handheld camera to emphasize the raw drama, he doesn't think the technique should be used as a crutch. "Another director might say, 'Move the camera so it looks energetic,'" Prieto says. "That's frankly something that I do not like. I try to have the camera move if the scene's energy makes it move."

What all the cinematographers have in common is their love of working with actors, and the special historic relationship between cinematographer and the actors continues undiminished. Actors are the most vulnerable participants on a film set, standing in front of the camera and performing while all around focus on them. The cinematographer can make their lives easier by ensuring that they look as good as they can, and making them feel comfortable. In the golden age of Hollywood, big name stars, especially actresses of a certain stature, would rely on the DP to make them shine. That relationship of trust and complicity still exists, sometimes even out of the director's earshot.

But the modern-day cinematographer has also to capture key moments of intimacy between actors without disrupting the moment. In the case of Kuras, who shot director Rebecca Miller's delicate **The Ballad of Jack and Rose**, the biggest compliment she could have asked for was when the film's star, Daniel Day-Lewis, told her that he never knew she was there, despite working together in such close quarters.

What was also striking about these acclaimed craftspeople was the amount of time and care they gave to discussing cinematography. In an era when most interviews with Hollywood talent are carefully manufactured affairs that are closely overseen by studios and publicists, resulting in bland sound bites wholly lacking in insight or depth, these DPs were enormously generous and lively, spending hours at restaurants, cafes, and their homes to discuss their training, their influences and their philosophies. In the case of the great Spanish cinematographer Javier Aguirresarobe, responsible for the gorgeous romanticism of **Vicky Cristina Barcelona** and the nightmarish post-apocalyptic landscapes of **The Road**, he insisted on having a translator present so that he could better articulate his thoughts in his native language. For Ed Lachman, who has worked with Steven Soderbergh and Todd Haynes, the interview included instances in which he consulted a handwritten journal that included jotted-down talking points he wanted to make sure to bring up.

The urgency these individuals brought to the discussion of cinematography was, in part, an attempt to clear up misconceptions about their craft. While they could talk about types of lenses and other technical jargon, a prevailing sentiment was that, in the end, such discussion must take a backseat to an intuitive, emotional response to the material and to the performances. Perhaps no other job on a film shoot is so evenly divided between the technical and the creative as a DP's. A common thread among our interview subjects was a belief that an understanding of the tools of filmmaking was essential, but only because once one learned that aspect of the job it could be put away so that the more important artistic demands could be addressed fully.

The cinematographers we interviewed came from a range of backgrounds. Though they shared a love of film in their youth, they also had divergent interests, including being captains of sports teams, or political junkies, or special-effects hobbyists, or impassioned shutterbugs. Some went to film school, while others studied anthropology or mathematics. Collectively, though, these DPs speak to the fact that any aspiring artist must draw from the cumulative experiences of his or her own life. For Caleb Deschanel, who was raised a Quaker, lensing **The Passion of the Christ** was less about the film's religious implications than it was about the storytelling. "I didn't have any real teachings about Jesus and the Bible," he said. "For me, it was this great dramatic story of the hero sacrificing himself for the betterment of others." Another DP would have approached the film from a different perspective, but it was Deschanel's unique slant on the material that made it so astounding.

2011 is a fascinating time to be talking to some of the world's greatest cinematographers. Technological change has impacted the creation of the moving image, not just in the emergence of digital cameras, but in the arrival of 3D technology, both as a means of shooting movies and in post-production in a conversion process from 2D to 3D.

DPs who might have initially sworn never to abandon film, or scoffed at shooting with a 3D camera, are frequently now experimenting with the new technology as it becomes easier to use and delivers a higher quality result. Doyle had just come off shooting his first 3D film—Takashi Shimizu's **Tormented**—in Japan when we spoke to him, and his experience was revelatory. He fast adapted to the camera and shot as he would normally. "I was astonished how beautiful it was, because it defied all the prejudices I have against 3D films," he said, adding that his chief agenda on the film was to avoid the technology becoming central to the process and keep the story and performance at the heart of the film.

Indeed, while all the interviewees speak of their flirtations and experiments with new technology, the *raison d'être* for a DP is to serve the story and the director. Yes, the subjects in this book are brimming with artistic passion and bright personalities but, while on set, they remain devoted, perhaps subservient, to the vision driving the film. At one time or another in the interviews, all of them referred to story as everything and even their boldest experiments with lighting or darkness were specific to what the film was trying to express or evoke.

The partnership with directors, of course, is essential in this regard and most of the cinematographers in the book have multiple films under their belt with certain filmmakers. Vittorio Storaro has worked extensively with Bernardo Bertolucci, Francis Ford Coppola, Warren Beatty, and Carlos Saura in his long career; Prieto with Alejandro González Iñárritu; Peter Suschitzky with David Cronenberg; and Christopher Doyle with Wong Kar-wai. They develop a professional shorthand with their directors, often lifelong friendships as well, which is sometimes wordless, sometimes argumentative, and usually results in a visual richness that perfectly combines their talents with the requirements of each narrative.

It was notable as we met the cinematographers and talked to them about their craft and work that there is a great sense of community at this top tier of the profession. Storaro recalled how Chris Menges had approached him when he was shooting **Agatha** in London in 1977 and expressed his desire to watch him at work; Menges worked as an operator on **Agatha** and later contributed to **Reds**. Menges himself told us that he had just returned from a visit to the set of Martin Scorsese's **Hugo** outside London to observe Robert Richardson shooting with 3D cameras. Menges meanwhile was a mentor of sorts to Barry Ackroyd, who shot a film Menges directed called **The Lost Son**; Menges also stepped in for his old friend Roger Deakins when Deakins had to leave the shooting of **The Reader** for a prior commitment. Seamus McGarvey told us that he called up Peter Suschitzky when he was struggling with an issue on the set of a film.

The network of connections, mentorships, and mutual support was especially exciting to hear and it extends to younger cinematographers. In his conversation, the colorful and outspoken Doyle urged young DPs to work with what they've got, even if that is shooting their surroundings for a YouTube clip. "They shouldn't try to make stories at first," he advised. "They should try to make some response to their environment and engage with it."

Also common to these master cinematographers is a hectic travel schedule. Indeed, one suspects that a comfort with being on the road is a vital pre-requisite for this craft. Menges was just preparing to fly from his home in Wales to New York City for four months to shoot **Extremely Loud and Incredibly Close** for director Stephen Daldry; McGarvey was in LA when we caught him en route from New York (where he had shot **We Need to Talk About Kevin** for Lynne Ramsay) to New Mexico for six months on the comic book epic **The Avengers** with Joss Whedon; Ackroyd was heading out of London to New Orleans to work on the thriller **Contraband** with Baltasar Kormákur. Beebe had just spent eight months in New Orleans on **Green Lantern**. Doyle was in Hong Kong en route from Japan to Austria via Los Angeles. The travel requirements are dizzying.

Throughout the project, the names of great innovators and pioneers in the craft kept popping up and that is why five cinematographers are profiled for their legacy. Gregg Toland, Freddie Young, Jack Cardiff, Sven Nykvist, and Raoul Coutard changed the medium through their films, and their work is the touchstone for many cinematographers working today. The legacy chapters aim to show why they made a difference and why they still matter today. The first four of those legacy subjects are no longer with us; Raoul Coutard is 86 and lives in France and, although he hasn't shot a film in over a decade, is probably the most influential DP alive today.

In our final choices of interviewees, we wanted to include a breadth of different styles and tastes, a range of different ages, and representations of different filmmaking cultures and budget ranges. Sixty years ago, The Academy released a promotional short film called **The Cinematographer**, which offered a breezy introduction to this crucial profession in the movie industry. The short concluded with the unnamed voiceover actor proudly intoning, "The cinematographer, the director of photography, has but one purpose: to add to your movie-going pleasure by giving you what you want to see—top entertainment in pictures." Though entertainment continues to be part of the equation, it's a sign of how much filmmaking has evolved that a cinematographer's role isn't so simple anymore. These dedicated artists challenge us, move us, astound us, and show us our world in ways we couldn't possibly have imagined. They usually communicate through images: This book allows them to speak to us directly in their own words.

In addition to each of the inspiring subjects, many people deserve thanks for helping to put this book together, notably the editorial team at Ilex Press led by Natalia Price-Cabrera and Zara Larcombe.

Thanks should also go to the representatives who helped facilitate access to their clients: Lynda Mamy at United Agents, Catherine Disabato at Dattner Dispoto & Associates, David Gersh and Kevin Rowe at The Gersh Agency, Paul Hook and Nikolas Palchikoff at ICM, Wayne Fitterman and Ryan Tracey at UTA, Julia Kole and Miranda Peters at The Julia Kole Agency, Kate Bloxham at Casarotto, Tom Marquardt and Michael Kirschner at ICM, Craig Bernstein at ICM, Heather Salazar at 42West, Kim Weston at the American Society Of Cinematographers, Angela Carbonetti of Parseghian Planco, and John Baumgartner.

Other thanks to Susan Stoebner, Elinor Actipis and Anais Wheeler at Focal Press.

Mike Goodridge
Tim Grierson
Oct 2011

Vilmos Zsigmond

"I really think the lighting is the most important
element in the movies. Without good lighting,
I don't think there's good cinematography."

One of the most influential cinematographers in the medium, Vilmos Zsigmond was born in Hungary in 1930. He studied cinema at the Academy of Drama and Film in Budapest, received an MA in cinematography in 1955, and then worked as assistant cameraman, operator, and director of photography at Hunnia Film Studio. During the 1956 Hungarian Revolution, he and his friend László Kovács were among the cameramen chronicling the dramatic events in Budapest, smuggling the footage out of the country and into Austria.

Zsigmond and Kovács moved to the US and settled in Los Angeles, where Zsigmond found work in photo labs as a technician and photographer. During the 1960s, using the name William Zsigmond, he shot a number of low-budget cult horror movies including **The Sadist** (1963), **The Nasty Rabbit** (1964), and **The Incredibly Strange Creatures Who Stopped Living and Became Mixed-Up Zombies** (1964).

On the advice of Peter Fonda, his director on **The Hired Hand** (1971), he returned to his original name and throughout the 1970s shot some of the most significant films of the era: **McCabe & Mrs. Miller** (1971), **Images** (1972), and **The Long Goodbye** (1973) for Robert Altman, **Deliverance** (1972) for John Boorman, **Scarecrow** (1973) for Jerry Schatzberg, and Steven Spielberg's first feature **The Sugarland Express** (1974).

The 1970s also saw him win an Oscar for Spielberg's **Close Encounters of the Third Kind** (1977), begin long collaborations with Brian De Palma and Mark Rydell, and shoot two seminal masterpieces with Michael Cimino—**The Deer Hunter** (1978) and **Heaven's Gate** (1980).

He has worked at the highest level since, alongside directors including Richard Donner, Phillip Noyce, Sean Penn, Kevin Smith, and Woody Allen, for whom he shot **Melinda and Melinda**, **Cassandra's Dream**, and **You Will Meet a Tall Dark Stranger**.

Vilmos Zsigmond

"I started out in the US doing a lot of low-budget movies on two-perf Techniscope like **The Nasty Rabbit** and **The Incredibly Strange Creatures**. We shot them on 35mm 100- to 150-feet "short ends," of 35mm color negative, which were sold by studios for one fifth of the price. The expense was less than shooting on 16mm.

I was lucky, because I was around when all these young filmmakers came up who didn't want to do the old-style Hollywood movies. The Hollywood movie was all Technicolor, musicals or westerns—very predictable types of films. They were searching for new guys to shoot them and we were the new guys. Get those crazy Hungarians who work for nothing!

László Kovács and I shot films in different ways because of our European background. In Hungary we grew up on Russian movies and Italian neorealist movies because we were allowed to see anything that made capitalism look bad. They were fresh and dealt with social problems. And then there was the New Wave, of course, which made a lot of changes to the tradition, telling stories about people.

In the 1970s it was the golden era for young filmmakers. The independent film movement started and these films were very low budget. I think Gene Hackman and Al Pacino worked for a very low salary on **Scarecrow**; they probably made $10,000 a week plus a small percentage. The budget on **Obsession** was around $900,000.

I don't know if I have a style. If I had the same style on every movie, it wouldn't be interesting. My style is to tell the story the right way each time. Sometimes that's a conservative style with classic lighting, like **Close Encounters of the Third Kind**. Or **The Deer Hunter** where we were aiming for reality. Or **McCabe & Mrs. Miller** where I destroyed the film by making it grainy and old like the old West. I pushed the film, and flashed it using fog filters to diffuse everything, so

THE DEER HUNTER

(01–02) The Deer Hunter was shot and lit in three separate and distinct styles by Zsigmond—the steel mill section at home in Pennsylvania, the Vietnam sequences, and the return to the United States. The first section, says Zsigmond, was "just normal. It was beautiful but there was a sort of romantic quality to working in the steel mill, all the orange light from the steel mixed with the blue light. It was influenced by Storaro who started using that effect—inside the room is warm (orange) and outside is cold (blue). The Vietnam section had a very newsreel quality to it to the point that we had to match actual 16mm newsreel footage from the war in order to tell the story. We couldn't recreate some of that ourselves, so we had to destroy the 35mm negative in order to match it to the 16mm footage."

The third section was designed as very somber and desaturated. "We wanted it black-and-white-ish and harsh; we used a no-diffusion filter," says Zsigmond.

it would look old, almost bad. The studio hated that film. They wanted to fire me. They said, "Fire that son of a bitch, he doesn't know what he's doing. He can't even expose the film right."

I love *film noir* style because that's dramatic; it's visual, and the images and the lighting tell the story. Almost all my movies use a *film noir* type of lighting, which is hard direct light sources. I don't like soft lighting—it might be natural but it's not exciting. I don't like to bounce lights into the ceiling and light the whole set. Painters never lit their work with soft light, they always had source lighting from windows or candles. If I can't do the same, I am not happy because then anybody could do the job.

I really think the lighting is the most important element in a movie. Without good lighting, I don't think there's good cinematography.

I want to be able to contribute to a project and use my experience with lighting, setting up the camera, and designing the movement. I like to work together with the director to establish the style of the movie and stick to it. Directional lighting takes a little longer than soft lighting. In order to light the set properly, I need to find four or five different positions for the lights. I like the actors to go in and out of the lights. I think that gives you a third dimension in the two-dimensional world of cinema.

In 2D you have to create the depth. That's the beauty of it, the art of it. That's why I think using a 3D camera to tell a story doesn't work. It's a technical gimmick that will die because, ultimately, people want to be absorbed in the story.

I don't like this trend today either of handheld camera. It's not my cup of tea. I find it too obtrusive. When the camera is shaking all over the place, you cannot forget that you are watching a movie. I don't like that. I want people to watch the film and forget themselves and feel like they are there. I'm a realist; I suppose if you want to be general about my style, you'd call it poetic realism. It's not the real thing. It's more real than real. There is some poetry in it. →

Shooting the rapids

(01–02) Zsigmond describes the **Deliverance** shoot in Alabama as "a great adventure." "We shot long lens most of the time, with a telephoto lens on the rapids sequences. We figured out what was the most exciting way for the audience to feel how treacherous those rapids were and how you could die there. The long lens keeps the actors very close to you and it gives you the speed of those boats. We figured out that panning the camera gives you more speed than going with them. And going parallel with people on the boat is not as exciting as using a long lens and putting the camera at body level so that we have that strange angle, like shooting from a low angle into a distance—that gives you tremendous speed."

I know how to work with directors. I know what their challenges are and I seldom have arguments with them because I am trying to shoot their ideas and not mine. There are cinematographers who want to take over the director's job by insisting on trying their way first. I don't like that. Directors should be directors and we should give them the freedom to do what they want. Even if it's wrong, the director has the right to be wrong. Of course I will come up with suggestions, but the director has a choice to take them or not.

On first meeting, you have to find out if you are really made for each other. It's almost like a marriage—you have to find out how the director likes to work and how your combined efforts would work. And if I feel like we won't be able to work together because he or she likes to do everything—set up the camera, choose the lenses, even operate the camera—I will walk away. Stanley Kubrick used to work that way. Of course, he was a genius and got away with it.

Spielberg was a young guy when we did **The Sugarland Express**, but very talented. Even then I knew he was a genius. He wanted me to shoot **Jaws**, but I decided not to do it because, honestly, I didn't like the script. I like to shoot films about people, not animals. But if I had done **Jaws**, I probably would not have done **Close Encounters**, and I was lucky to wait for that one.

> "Directors should be directors and we should give them the freedom to do what they want. Even if it's wrong, the director has the right to be wrong."

It was a huge production, with huge problems and budget issues. Steven wanted to have better and better things than were planned, and we started to run out of money. Columbia Pictures were scared to death and felt that they were on the brink of a financial catastrophe, so it was pretty tough. They were blaming me for a lot of it—for using too many lights.

We did use a lot of light. There were no digital effects in those days. We had to create very bright light effects on the floor from the spaceships that would be added later in post-production. They turned out so well that even today we couldn't do any better. In the landing area at the end of the film, the set was so big that we had about 300 10K lights together to create the effect of one big light with one shadow on the floor. It was expensive stuff, and not budgeted.

Special-effects designer Douglas Trumbull was a great help to me. He kept explaining to the producers and studio executives why we had to have those bright effects done for real on the set with so many lights. Steven Spielberg stood behind us too, knowing that we were going to end up with the great look necessary for the ending of the movie. →

> "I operated the camera in the early days because I didn't know how to shoot movies any other way. I couldn't tell my operator what to do because a lot of the time film is improvisation."

François Truffaut enjoyed working with us. One day he was standing next to me looking at the hundreds of lamps above and said: "Vilmos, you know for the money you guys are spending in one day here on set, I could shoot ten movies in France."

Brian DePalma is easy to work with, as he knows exactly what he wants. He also believes that the cinematographer can help to make a movie look better and help it become more successful, and accepts the collaboration of all departments. He lets me set up the camera, enjoys watching me lighting the set, and depends on me to deal with the laboratory on timing the density and color of the dailies and the intermediate process.

He's a very creative director. Once in a while he wants one of his "signature" 360- or 720-degree circular dolly shots, which are difficult to light. It's always a joy to come up with the solution to where to hide the lights to get the dramatic effect he is looking for. It's fun to work with him.

On **The Bonfire of the Vanities**, the opening shot was a five-minute Steadicam shot which we prepared in one day and shot the second. We didn't have 500-feet rolls because strangely enough, while Panavision makes 500 magazines, Kodak doesn't make 500-feet rolls. So we had to break 1000-feet rolls into 500s, which meant we often ran out of film before we got to the end of the scene. Out of 12 takes we only got the full scene six or seven times. Brian insisted on having the scene in one shot, without cuts.

I operated the camera in the early days because I didn't know how to shoot movies any other way. I couldn't tell my operator what to do because, a lot of the time, film is improvisation. Altman, for example, loved to improvise, and when I am behind the camera, I can improvise myself, hand on the zoom. I learned how to use the zoom from Altman because he was excellent at designing shots with the zoom and the dolly. Altman knew a lot about cameras. When he did dollies with zoom, he hid the fact that he was using a zoom lens. →

McCABE & MRS. MILLER
(01–04) To create the feeling of age, Zsigmond used fog filters to push the film to make it seem old and grainy. (01) Left to right: David Foster, producer; Tommy Thompson, assistant director; Vilmos Zsigmond and Robert Altman.

THE ROSE

(01–02) To shoot Bette Midler's concert footage in Mark Rydell's **The Rose**, Zsigmond enlisted a group of his cinematographer friends to work the cameras at the Hollywood Bowl. Haskell Wexler, John A. Alonzo, Owen Roizman, and his operator Michael Margulies. "They didn't get paid, but they loved doing it," recalls Zsigmond. "I didn't have to tell them what to shoot, I just cut them loose and said do anything you like. Haskell was in the Far East and arrived back in Los Angeles and didn't go home; he came straight from the airport to the concert. He didn't want to miss it." **(02)** The crew with Vilmos Zsigmond (pointing) and director Mark Rydell at the camera.

"...as a cinematographer you have to embrace new technology, if only because producers think it's cheaper to shoot digital."

I love composition in the widescreen format. The anamorphic format is really perfect and it helps the editing because you have to cut less in an anamorphic movie. You have a closeup in the front left and a long shot in the right on the other side, so even if it's a little out of focus, you have the environment in the same shot as the closeup. If you are shooting TV, a closeup is a closeup. You don't see anything else. It's not exciting or visual. That's why I think there is a renaissance happening in anamorphic movies.

I find digital photography a bit boring because of the 16:9 format. It's not as exciting as 2:40:1 and lots of people actually have to go back to film and shoot in anamorphic to make it more visually interesting. I shot with a RED camera in Hungary recently and the colors look great when you are watching the dailies, but when you go to post-production, something is lost. Having said that, I am sure it will get much better and as a cinematographer you have to embrace new technology, if only because producers think it's cheaper to shoot digital. On bigger budget films, however, I would stay away from digital and stick to film. It's still hard to beat.

YOU WILL MEET A TALL DARK STRANGER; CASSANDRA'S DREAM

Zsigmond says that Woody Allen is "not into the camera too much." "I always have to bring him to look through the lens," he says. "He's not interested in that. It's about story and actors for him. There's not much you can do with the visuals. Lighting is important and he fell in love with the Steadicam on **You Will Meet a Tall Dark Stranger** (01). There's a scene between Josh Brolin, Naomi Watts, and Gemma Jones in the house where we shot in a hallway, living room, and kitchen, and in one shot you see all these rooms. We kept the shot together for four minutes and you're not bored watching it because it's so well staged." (02) Vilmos Zsigmond, center left, with Woody Allen, center right, at Paddington Station during the filming of **Cassandra's Dream**.

HEAVEN'S GATE

(01–04) Although notorious for bringing down a movie studio (United Artists), Michael Cimino's **Heaven's Gate** is now considered a masterpiece. "When you do a movie about the past like that, you have to do it quite painterly, because if it's too realistic by today's standards, it loses something," he says. "It has to feel like you are in the past."

Christopher Doyle

"The cinematographer is the closest person to the actor. We are his or her first audience, so we have to be responsive, responsible, and a trusted confidante, because the more engaged we are, the more the audience will be engaged."

One of the world's most audacious and brilliant cinematographers, Christopher Doyle was born in 1952 in Australia, but has spent most of his professional life in Asia. Prior to his first DP job in 1983, he had worked as an oil driller, a cow herder, and a doctor of Chinese medicine, but it was his 8mm and video work that inspired Taiwan's Edward Yang to hire him for his debut film **That Day, on the Beach**. Fluent in Mandarin, Doyle subsequently found himself a popular cinematographer in Hong Kong and China.

In 1990, he shot the second feature film from up-and-coming Hong Kong director Wong Kar-wai, **Days of Being Wild**, which began a collaboration between the two that included some of the most iconic Asian films of the next two decades: **Chungking Express** and **Ashes of Time** in 1994, **Fallen Angels** in 1995, **Happy Together** in 1997, **In the Mood for Love** in 2000, **2046** in 2004, and Wong Kar-wai's segment of **Eros—The Hand**—in 2004. He also worked as cinematographer for Chen Kaige on **Temptress Moon** (1996), Zhang Yimou on **Hero** (2002), and Fruit Chan on **Dumplings** (2004), as well as producing Zhang Yuan's **Beijing Bastards** (1993).

As his fame spread, filmmakers around the world sought out Doyle to shoot their movies and he has worked with names as diverse as Gus Van Sant (**Psycho** and **Paranoid Park**), Jim Jarmusch (**The Limits of Control**), Barry Levinson (**Liberty Heights**), Phillip Noyce (**Rabbit-Proof Fence** and **The Quiet American**), M. Night Shyamalan (**Lady in the Water**), James Ivory (**The White Countess**) and Neil Jordan (**Ondine**). He has made films all over Asia including **Last Life in the Universe** and **Invisible Waves** with Pen-Ek Ratanaruang in Thailand. In 2011, he completed his first 3D production, **Tormented**, in Japan with Takashi Shimizu and the German/Japanese co-production **Underwater Love**, a "Pinkyu" genre musical. He wrote, directed, and shot his own feature **Away with Words**, set in Hong Kong and Japan, and directed and shot **Warsaw Dark**, a Polish production in Polish, despite it being a language he doesn't speak. He has produced several books, including *Why I Am Not a Painter* and *Picture Start*.

Christopher Doyle

"Hopefully the function of what we do gives resonance to the image. The function of the cinematographer is to be the bridge, the conduit between the audience and what's in front of the camera. To me there are only three people in cinema: the person in front of the camera, the audience member, and the person who is the real passage between them—the cinematographer. Of course there is a logistical structure, and a director and producer to facilitate the interface. But for the engagement to be direct and compelling, I really believe we have to be transparent and remove ourselves enough so that the passage between the actors and audience is direct.

Most of the people I work with are friends and it's a relationship. I spent so many years of life with Wong Kar-wai and many other gifted, committed artists and why would you do it if you don't love them? Why would you spend six months—or four years in the case of **2046**— with someone you didn't share a vision and

commitment with? You see so many people who think they can further their so-called careers by working with assholes, and many western filmmakers are assholes. You have to cut them loose. No, it has to be a friendship to start with.

The directors don't know what the fuck to do with me most of the time. I guess I compromise them into being "indulgent." Hopefully something unexpected comes out of that. Wong Kar-wai always says "Is that all you can do, Chris?" And I think he is right. What he is saying is "I want more from you" and "Do you really think that's enough?" He knows that I can do more but you don't know what you can do unless you push yourself beyond what you thought were your limits. "Is that all you can do?" is an extremely important question and my answer is "It won't happen again." It has happened to me many times where you do exceed yourself, and it's because of the trust that actors give you, and the support of the crew.

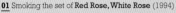

01 Smoking the set of **Red Rose, White Rose** (1994)

02 Setting up the Halloween scene in **Liberty Heights** (1999)

> **"My job is also to inform myself and the audience through visual experience and enhance it or suggest another visual experience."**

Of course, film is a whole group of people getting together to do something which is actually beyond even their own comprehension, hopefully bigger than oneself. It's written down but it's not expressed. When you find form in an image or a gesture or perhaps in the relationship between the camera and the space and the person within that space, it's astonishing. It was there all the time, but didn't come to light until you found it.

My job is also to inform myself and the audience through visual experience and enhance it or suggest another visual experience. I have used green moonlight in many of my films, not blue moonlight which is the convention. Blue moonlight comes from the past when they had oil-lamp floodlights which gave you a suggestion of night being comforting. One hundred years later on, people are still following this convention. But if you go to Venice or if you look at the Pacific, moonlight is not blue, it is green. If you are in LA

or London, the sky is tinged with orange light from the incandescent lights that illuminate the city. You have to record that visual experience and share it. Moonlight can be green or it can be pink. The same thing applies to other conventions, such as certain camera movements, or the consistency of light sources—even a so-called "seamless" edit. Art is supposed to transcend the mundane, the accepted, not condescend to it.

If you are working with digital media, such as a cellphone camera or the Internet or even 3D, the energy and the challenge comes from applying the peculiarities of the medium, not trying to replicate the tone qualities or conventions of film. Derek Jarman's eye responded to and exploited the grain, contrast, and random response of the 8mm camera's iris to light changes to create works of great beauty with the simplest of means.

I have basically been a foreigner more than three quarters of my life and you have to be an →

HERO

(01–07) Zhang Yimou's epic martial arts saga **Hero** is one of Doyle's richest achievements and he describes it as a gift, since the film used different colors to tell different parts of the story. "It's a film that gives color an active narrative role, far beyond its symbolic or emotional function," he says. Doyle won the New York Film Critics Circle award for cinematography as well as the Hong Kong Film Award in 2003 for his work. "I went totally crazy in **Hero**," he says. "How can you make a film about color? What an incredibly generous thing for Zhang Yimou, who is an ex-cinematographer, to give a

cinematographer. I asked him what it was about and he said 'color.' The theme of the film was color and he had the vision to push it through. I was scared out of my head making it. You would walk into these huge blue rooms which didn't seem real. But ultimately I believed in the colors and the light, and the audience did too." Images **01–03** (opposite) show some of Doyle's own abstractions of the material from the shoot.

"I assume in any film community in the world, I'm regarded as a little bit eccentric, but that's OK."

outsider from the inside if you want to be a cinematographer. You have to be close enough to the experience, but removed enough to see it in another way. That is what art is about. I know Chinese society because I have lived in it, but I was born in another country. I am a white guy in a yellow world. I am not even Christopher Doyle, I am Dukefeng. That is extremely liberating. Why are so many of the great cinematographers in America non-American? Anthony Dod Mantle makes Danish films—he is British; Tim Burton and Terry Gilliam are just as inspired even living in village London. Only when you are looking from the outside will you see stuff that resonates, which people understand but have never seen until then.

In Hong Kong, *gweilo* means ghost and usually it's an insult for white people in the Hong Kong community. When Wong Kar-wai or others talk about *gweilo* on a Hong Kong film set everyone knows they are talking about no one but me. I am extremely honored by that. They know I am a little different, but for some reason, they are stuck with me. I assume in any film community in the world, I'm regarded as a little bit eccentric, but that's OK. It means only the crazies actually call me—people of some like-mindedness or mutual intent.

I always operate my own camera. Always. Everyone knows that, even the unions. My contracts state I am director of photography, and I am camera operator. When we did **Temptress Moon**, the director asked if his best mate could operate the camera. Traditionally, visitors bring gifts of whisky and fruit to Chinese sets. In my anxiety and frustration I finished a good bottle →

IN THE MOOD FOR LOVE

(01–04) Doyle's work on **In the Mood for Love** is often cited as his greatest, but he attributes the success of the film to the actors Tony Leung and Maggie Cheung. "I don't know how to say this politely but the greatest actors I have ever worked with and with whom I have greatest afinity have all been Asian," he says. "I don't know how they do it. There is no entourage, no pretense. Tony and Maggie will be joking behind the scenes before they go on, they won't need to work out their motivation. I tried to create a certain ambience, but really we were just responding to these incredible actors." From Doyle's archive: Maggie Cheung in her closet (01) and through the viewfinder (02).

Working with Wong Kar-wai

(01–03) Wong Kar-wai often doesn't have a screenplay for his films but works through a process of experimentation and improvisation. Doyle says that in preparation for each of the films, Wong Kar-wai would get Doyle and his other chief collaborators to focus on music and literature. "It was always about music, and often about literature, but nothing related to the film itself," says Doyle. "We both read a lot of Puig, Fuentes, Borges, and then he would play some music and say that is what he was thinking about for the film. I wouldn't have a fucking idea what it meant but the challenge to respond intuitively, to take the energy of the music or the narrative twist did inform the image in some subconscious way. He played me some Frank Zappa for **Happy Together** and said that is what the scene should look like. Wong Kar-wai is not conventional. His film is not like a BMW commercial. He makes you take something away from the music and make it your own and bring back to the film what you can. There is an understanding. The same with (production designer and editor) William Chang Suk-ping. The first time we worked together on **Days of Being Wild**, I said I thought the film should have a lot of green and William opened the warehouse door and showed me a whole room full of green and tangerine-colored dresses. You know you are in the right space. We don't need to talk when we look at locations. We don't even say anything. We just walk in and don't even know what scene it is for and just say yes or no. That understanding doesn't come from verbal communication."

01 Montage by Doyle: Wong Kar-wai on the set of **2046**

02 2046

03 Fallen Angels

"Most of the films I have done have limited budgets, so you do what you can, not what you want."

and a case of oranges watching and trying to get someone else to do something I couldn't communicate, and yet I knew exactly how to do. Operating the camera is intrinsic to how I work. I have to operate because I don't think I want to have an idea translated or reinterpreted, I just want to do it. It's not getting from A to B that counts, it's how you get there. Otherwise it's too far removed from the process for me and if you are not engaging with the person in front of the camera, how can you articulate something that you want to share with the audience?

There are a few of us like that—Rodrigo Prieto, Anthony Dod Mantle, Rain Li—most who started in no-budget, do-it-all-yourself-because-you-care films. We are camera people, not Directors of Photography. In Britain or America or China, the relationship between the camera and the DP is traditionally more removed and more conjectural, and supposedly more objective. But I don't trust that objectivity. It may work for certain kinds of processes, but it's just not get-your-hands-dirty or visceral enough for me.

I want to light my own set as well. I want to feel the physicality. I want to be close to the actors because I believe that is the intimacy we need. The directness of communications. It's about authorship. I want this film to look like a film I made.

I don't think lighting is everything. I believe location and climate are everything. On **Last Life in the Universe**, we found an old dilapidated villa, an hour out of Bangkok. And I knew when I saw this house that this was the third character in the film, this is what the film was about.

Most of the films I have done have limited budgets, so you do what you can, not what you want. You don't impose a style. Going back to Wong Kar-wai, when you don't have a script, the style has to evolve from the state of the image that you work up. That is fundamental to how my own work has evolved. So as soon as I see a space, I make decisions: yes, no, yes, no. On a Wong Kar-wai film, that's all you have. It's basically the Feng Shui. The space implies certain possbilities. The position of elements attracts the body and eye to sit there and avoid

that corner. The light falls in a way that implies "peace" or "anxiety" so you respond to that and perhaps enhance it a little. Feng Shui informs intent.

You couldn't even stand in the entrance to the apartment in **In the Mood for Love**, for example, and yet somehow the space engages you in a certain way. One of the pluses of working with Wong Kar-wai was never knowing what was going to work and what was not going to work. You had to base people in the space. You respond to a situation, and then how the camera responds to those people in that space, and then the so-called style comes from that.

I hope this attitude, this approach, is encouraging to younger filmmakers because, if they really want to make films that is probably all they will have. They will have a shitty little camera with shitty resolution and no detail, but if they regard this or the ability of inexperienced actors or lack of lunch money as a limitation they are missing the point. "There are no problems, there are only solutions" might sound a little like a Starbucks cliché, but don't let "the eyes be higher than the hand" as they say in Chinese. Do what you can. Don't get stuck on what you want, and then when you find a crack in the possible go through it. It's your crack—"that's how the light gets in" Leonard Cohen assures us. And the way the light gets in and the way you respond to it will be unique, and only yours. Don't try and imitate others, certainly don't try to imitate Christopher Doyle. The only reason to make films is because we have something to say, to articulate our personalities.

I've done many commercials where people say I want it to look like some of the films you've done. It never does. I think all they mean to say is that they have a feeling for my work. You can't storyboard the way a film should look. Because once you have been on a set and it starts to rain and an actor is not performing in the way you expected, you have to wing it. It has to be based on experience and understanding; working out how to get past the negative energy you are feeling at the time, or the bad weather you are having, or

PSYCHO

(01–03) When Gus Van Sant wanted to make a scene-by-scene remake of Alfred Hitchcock's **Psycho**, he recruited Doyle as his cinematographer. "**Psycho** is not a film, it's a PhD in art theory, it's conceptual art," laughs Doyle. "The film is a by-product, not the motivator. That is what **Psycho** is to me. That Hollywood would have given us $20m to make an art project is astonishing. Gus is a genius for knowing that is what it was about. It was about acknowledging a master and sharing with another generation what the essence of purity is. It's about discovering what makes art work."

Doyle said that by making the film color, he was faced with numerous challenges about the meaning of color in a western society. "In the black-and-white version, she has a white bra on before she steals the money and a black bra afterwards. That is part of American Christian symbolism and our challenge of **Psycho** was to give color to the symbolic values of Judeo-Christian heritage.

I live in the East and white is the color of death in Asia, not the color of purity as it is in the West. So the beauty of our process is that we can interpret or redefine the resonance of ideas through color. We ended with pink as pure and green as trangression. I am not sure that these choices are transcendent or profound, they just said something to us. And that's all they had in the bra store that wasn't polka-dotted or lacey anyway.

the fact that everyone is hungry or drunk.

I had no idea what I was doing on my first film with Edward Yang and it was fantastic. That is how I live and work, even now. It is great to be out of your depth and not have any idea because that actually makes you courageous enough to make the mistakes that show you what is possible. I think mistakes are wondrous things. They teach you so much.

A simple example. On **Fallen Angels**, we had one scene where the film stock was totally underexposed. We didn't know what went wrong, it looked like it had been through a washing machine. So we said, why don't we change it to black and white, and then if we have one scene which is black and white, why don't we have a few more scenes that are black and white? So we basically tried to compensate for a technical fuck-up and it became a stylistic innovation. And then when we got to do **Happy Together**, Wong Kar-wai started out making three minutes at the beginning in black and white and then it became 20 minutes. What is supposedly a mistake becomes a possibility.

I was very honored when Neil Jordan told me that all my films look different. I didn't know →

"I am anti-intellectual about the process because I think that once you start intellectualizing, you scare the kids away from making their own mistakes."

that, and my only response was that we did them in different places with different people. I wasn't being facetious or naïve or arrogant. I really believed that's what happened.

If you aspire to something greater than yourself, others will step up to it. It's beautiful to watch. Our job is to be real people open to the possibilities that the process of filmmaking offers and hire good people who know what they are doing. You have to assume the role. It's master and commander. The master is the director and the commander is the cinematographer, but you can have really good shipmates.

I am an anti-intellectual about the process because I think once you start intellectualizing, you scare the kids away from making their own mistakes. It also implies that we are above everyone else. I despise the hierarchy and sense of privilege, and the implication that it takes so much research and effort and correct knowledge to be what we are. I disagree. I happened into what I am doing. I am not an art student. Apparently I am partly color blind. I was never an assistant. Someone just gave me a camera and I am here.

01

02

RABBIT-PROOF FENCE

(01–03) Phillip Noyce's highly acclaimed 2002 film **Rabbit-Proof Fence** told the story of Aborigine girls escaping from white re-education camps in 1931 Australia, and Doyle won plaudits for his stark, desaturated color images of the Outback. "We were two white fellas daring to make one of the most important black Australian stories," recalls Doyle. "We had to be humble, and approach the history with respect, and focus on what it meant to the people involved. We had mostly Aboriginal crew, so their rhythm and intent is basic to how the film is and looks." (03) Photo frottage of the film by Doyle.

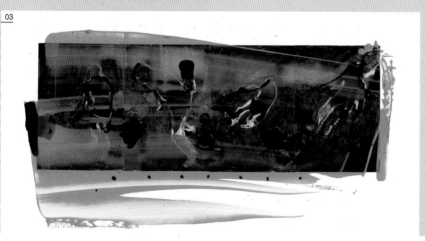
03

Working in 3D

Doyle had a positive experience shooting his first film with 3D cameras, Takashi Shimizu's horror film **Tormented (01–04)** despite initial skepticism.

Be open-minded: "I tried to watch **Avatar** 20 times but couldn't get through more than five minutes. But when I made the film in 3D, I was astonished at how beautiful it was, and none of my prejudices about 3D films came true. Of course, we had a team who knew about 3D, as did the director himself, but the 3D isn't in your face. It looks like a film that happens to be in 3D. I worked closely with people who knew what they were doing with the 3D so when, in my ignorance, I would ask 'What if we did this?' together we found something even better."

Focus on the story, don't get caught up in the 3D: Doyle says that he didn't even look at the playback each day because he wanted to remove himself as much as possible from the "3D-ness" of it: "I watched the final edit with my glasses on, but I was looking as I do on any film at composition, the relationship between performance and camera, and how we articulated emotion or someone got from A to B."

Learn where 3D will work, and where it won't: "3D now is like a zoom lens was in the 1960s. Now many of us use a zoom lens more as a variable-focal lens, a quick way to get to a composition that works for you, much more discretely than the showiness a zoom was when it was first introduced. I couldn't imagine that 3D could last more than another ten years before I did this film. As we learn its strengths and pitfalls, the medium, like digital imagery or animation, starts to celebrate its function and develop its own particular visual and emotional voice."

Michael Ballhaus

"With movement you can express a lot of things. Sometimes, motion is emotion—you can create emotion by moving the camera."

In a career that has extended from his native Germany to the United States, Michael Ballhaus has been celebrated for fluid camerawork and artful compositions that are always in service to the many types of films he has shot. Coming of age at the dawn of the New German Cinema movement, Ballhaus enjoyed a creatively fruitful (though personally contentious) relationship with director Rainer Werner Fassbinder, which began with **Whity** (1971) and culminated in **The Marriage of Maria Braun** (1979). From there, he ventured to America and worked with emerging filmmakers such as John Sayles (**Baby It's You**, 1983), James Foley (**Reckless**, 1984) and Marisa Silver (**Old Enough**, 1984). But it was in 1985 when he would begin his second major collaborative relationship, this time with Martin Scorsese on **After Hours** (1985). The two men have gone on to film **The Color of Money** (1986), **The Last Temptation of Christ** (1988), **Goodfellas** (1990), **The Age of Innocence** (1993), **Gangs of New York** (2002) and **The Departed** (2006), which won the Best Picture Oscar. Ballhaus has been nominated for Academy Awards for his cinematography on **Broadcast News** (James L. Brooks, 1987), **The Fabulous Baker Boys** (Steve Kloves, 1989) and **Gangs of New York**. As adept with sophisticated comedy as he is with gothic horror, Ballhaus teamed up with Mike Nichols for **Working Girl** (1988) and helped create the looming sense of dread that envelops Francis Ford Coppola's adaptation of **Bram Stoker's Dracula** (1992).

Michael Ballhaus

"I grew up in the theater. My parents owned a theater company, which makes you definitely want to become an actor when it's the world that surrounds you. My parents were absolutely against it—they said, "First, you finish school and learn a real job, and if you still want to be an actor, then you can become an actor." But I learned that acting is a very hard job, so I decided to look for something else.

I started taking pictures when I was 15 years old, and I got good at it. I took all of the theater company's stage photos, and I liked it very much. But my first encounter with a movie set was on **Lola Montes**. My parents used to know Max Ophüls—they were friends. Being on a set was, for me, the moment of awakening—it was the combination of theater and taking pictures. I had started in photography, but once I saw what you could do with a film camera, I thought, "If I do moving images, I'll have to move the camera because otherwise I could just take pictures. These pictures

are moving." With movement you can express a lot of things. Sometimes, motion is emotion—you can create emotion by moving the camera.

There was no film school in those days—you had to learn by doing. To become a cinematographer in Germany, normally you become an assistant to a cinematographer, and if you got lucky then you could maybe become an operator. And then if you got really lucky, after ten years you could shoot your own movie. For me, it was different: I got a job at a TV station. I met some wonderful people who worked at the station and became friends with them. I shot my first feature when I was 25, so it was fairly fast. I needed very good gaffers and key grips and a good assistant—they helped me to get it right. I knew, basically, what I wanted—I just didn't know how to do it yet. But if you start doing it, then you'll learn.

My first movie was shot in Baden-Baden at the TV station, and the director was Peter Lilienthal. We just kind of started together—we developed

THE AGE OF INNOCENCE

(01–03) This was one of Ballhaus' favorite films to work on with Martin Scorsese. He uses the scene in the carriage, where Daniel Day Lewis touches Michelle Pfeiffer's glove and pulls it off (03), as an example to show his students when discussing the handling of erotic subjects.

They shot the opera scene (01) in the Music Hall in Philadelphia. The main difficulty was shooting the scenes in the theater boxes, because they had to film in an actual theater. The solution was to use a Technocrane, which stood on stilts over the seating below. "That didn't solve our problem, though, because it takes a lot of co-ordinating to operate a Technocrane. Three people were needed; one to swing the crane up and down, another to move it sideways, and the third to extend and retract the arm."

> **"I had done many more movies than Fassbinder—and he was a little bit intimidated by that. He always called me 'The TV Guy.'"**

the story and made storyboards and all that. I didn't know too much about the technical job of a cinematographer, but I knew a lot about storytelling. Normally when you become a cinematographer, you have to be an assistant for many years, and so it becomes first a technical job. For me, it was never technical—it was always a storytelling job. That had a lot to do with my upbringing in the theater—theater is a lot about storytelling, and that was what I loved.

I taught very early in my career—I was teaching at a film school in Berlin in '68. What was interesting is that I was forced to think about creative decisions. The students would ask, "Why did you do it this way? Why is the camera that high? Why are you using these lenses?" And you'd have to think about why you're doing it. So through teaching, I learned to explain why I was doing things, and that helped me a lot in my later career—I could always explain to directors why the shot looks like this or why I'm using these lenses.

When I first met Fassbinder, that was not so much fun. He didn't want a new DP, but the producer, who was a friend of mine, couldn't get the guy he wanted. So the producer recommended me because I had worked with him before. Fassbinder treated me very badly in the beginning. I had more experience—I had done many more movies than Fassbinder—and he was a little bit intimidated by that. He always called me "The TV Guy"—to him, I was the guy who had only done TV, and he wanted to make big movies. I thought, "This is not gonna last long." I never even unpacked my luggage. But then, slowly, it started getting better—not that he ever told me that he liked something I had done. After a screening once, he walked out and didn't say a word, but he later told our actor, Ulli Lommel, "This guy is fantastic." Of course, he never said a word to me.

Fassbinder always tried to give me very complicated shots to do and probably expected me to say, "I can't do it." But I never did that, →

AFTER HOURS

(01–02) This was Michael Ballhaus' first film with director Martin Scorsese, and chronicles one darkly comic night in the life of a lonely New Yorker trapped in an unfamiliar part of town. "I was daring enough to shoot almost wide-open with my lenses," Ballhaus recalls, "which probably none of my colleagues would have done. My focus puller was dying because depth of field was like nothing." But the decision was made because of the production's tight schedule. "I think we had 40 nights to shoot 600 shots," he says, "so that was the only way to do it quickly. We didn't have the money and the time to relight the streets, so we went with available light. That meant wide-open with high-speed stock—I mean, as fast as the stock was in those days. But I used very little light, and I had a very fast crew. They were all prepared—I told them before we started the night, 'OK, we have so many shots to do and we go in this order.'" The speed at which they shot forced Ballhaus "to make it fast, but not sloppy, so it still looks good." That could make for a delicate balancing act. "You could not be as perfect as you wanted to be, but when it's a story like **After Hours**, it can be a little

rough—it doesn't have to be perfectly lit. Besides, there was pressure every night—once it was five o'clock in the morning, the sky turned navy and that was it. It was time to go to bed." **(02)** Ballhaus filming **After Hours** in the rain.

> "Anything you can think, you can also do. Sometimes it takes a little longer, or it takes a little more money, but you can always do it."

because it was never in my head to say, "This is not possible." Anything you can think, you can also do. Sometimes it takes a little longer, or it takes a little more money, but you can always do it.

He had a very good sense of imagery—he told the story with images. That was something I liked a lot. There are directors who are more fascinated by dialogue and working with actors, and they don't care much about the images or the rhythm of the scene. He had the rhythm of the scene in his head—he knew shot-by-shot how the editing would work. Sometimes when we showed dailies, it looked like a rough cut. He knew exactly what he wanted. I worked for him for nine years and did 16 movies. He was a brilliant director, so I didn't care much how I was treated—I mean, sometimes it was bad and I wanted to quit, but he was the best director you could work with, so you put up with a lot of things. And, you know, nobody told me that this is an easy job and that you love every director and every director loves you.

When I started working in the States, I sometimes got offers to do action movies. And, you know, when you go to the movies, you like action sometimes. But I decided not to do action movies because sometimes the stories are a little more flat. I picked movies because of the directors and the kind of movies they liked, so most of the directors that I worked with, I liked the stories that they wanted to tell.

Once I got to America, I was again much more experienced than the director I was working with, John Sayles. But he knew that, and he gave me some freedom. On **Baby It's You**, he didn't tell me where to put the camera, or what lenses to use or how to light it—he just was very open and said, "What do you think?" I suggested shots, and he agreed to that. It was a very wonderful experience for me to see that you can work with a director in a different language in a different country and it still works the same way.

I was not perfectly fluent but pretty much fluent—I mean, I understood every word. I maybe couldn't express myself as elaborately as I learned to later, but I could explain myself, and I understood what he wanted. It did take me awhile to get jokes, though, because with jokes in a different language it's sometimes harder.

Now, when I started working with Scorsese, it was a totally different story because Marty had a very, very precise vision of his movies. He worked hard on his shot list, and when I got his shot list, I had a very clear idea how the movie should look. He's a very visual director, and that was a very important experience for me to work with somebody who had such a precise vision. His shot list was about the rhythm of a scene, the size, the movement, how it should look, how to light it, and what kind of lenses I should use. It was basically my job to transfer his ideas into images that go on screen.

Every movie Marty and I do, when we start we talk about the style—we talk about the colors. So on **Goodfellas**, we said, "OK, this is not a 'beautiful' movie—it's more like an ugly movie. It doesn't have to be perfectly lit." Also, we didn't have any famous stars that we had to light in a special, wonderful way, which you have to do when you do a movie like **The Age of Innocence** and you have someone like Michelle Pfeiffer and you have to make them look good because the story calls for it. For **Goodfellas**, while I still want Joe Pesci and Bob De Niro to look good, they were gangsters—it's more down-and-dirty.

I've shot both comedies and dramas, and it's very different. The timing of comedy is very, very important, and you've got to watch it carefully. You can't move the camera as much in a comedy as you can in drama because the timing is so crucial. I was lucky and got to work with good directors who have experience with comedy— I worked with Frank Oz on some of my favorite comedies, **What About Bob?** and **Dirty Rotten Scoundrels**. For comedies, the style changes totally, and you have to go with it because the shots are not as complicated as in a drama. If you move the camera a lot, you cannot edit it as simply as you need to—you're limited in terms of editing. So you need to make sure that the punch line is clear and that you can see everything you have to see. The shots should look beautiful, but →

THE LAST TEMPTATION OF CHRIST

(01–04) The shooting schedule and budget were extremely tight for this film, but Ballhaus managed to make it work. He was on location for eight weeks before shooting so he could plan every single shot in every location. He went to each place early in the morning and marked the position of the sun to determine at which point in time the light would be best. This way they managed to complete 36 set-ups on the first day.

Another problem was shooting the crowd scenes. "We could have used 500 extras but more than 150 simply wasn't possible. Yet, there were many moments where Scorsese was able to overcome these extremes and demonstrate his skill as a director. For example, the first time Jesus carries his cross, we shot at 120 frames per second using a very long lens, 300mm I think. The scene was inspired by Hieronymus Bosch." (02, 04) Pictures from Ballhaus' own archive of the shoot.

it's not about the images—it's more about the dialogue and the actors.

Creating a tone for a film can be a great challenge. If you have a period movie, like **Dracula**, where there was no electric light, you have to work with candles. A bulb is a constant light, but a fire is not a constant—it becomes brighter and darker and it flickers, and so all the lights are moving. And then you need a lot of darkness, because darkness is scary and dangerous. Then you need to find the right tone between seeing enough, but not too much. And then you have great costumes and great makeup and all these things. So, it was incredibly fascinating to do this movie, and we had some really fun ideas to do things a little different. We built something where we put the camera on a big handle that was hanging down from the ceiling,

and the camera was swinging up the stairs when Dracula approaches Mina's room. There were a lot of complicated, tricky things Francis Ford Coppola and I did in this one, and we prepared for that shoot for a long time and did all sorts of tests—it was very challenging. I'm surprised how good this movie is holding up, especially when you see it many, many years later. Sometimes when it's on television, I can never stop watching it. It still has a life.

Some faces are easier to light than others. When I did **Something's Gotta Give**, I had to do a lot of tests with our leading actress—she plays a person who is 60, but the director wanted her to look 40 and didn't want to see one wrinkle. That means we have to light her in a very, very specific way, so you do a lot of testing until you find out what the best way is. And if you get lucky, →

01–03 Ballhaus with Martin Scorsese on the set of **The Departed**

Games with Fassbinder

Michael Ballhaus' work with Rainer Werner Fassbinder on films like **The Marriage of Maria Braun** (01) and **The Bitter Tears of Petra von Kant** (02) is marked by its hypnotic, complicated tracking shots.

Creativity from conflict: That style, in part, was inspired by Fassbinder's combative relationship with the DP. "He didn't like to see the locations where he was shooting the scene," says Ballhaus. "He always relied on the production designer or me to pick out the locations, and then when we came on the set, he'd look at me and say, 'OK, so, you picked this location—why? How would you do it?' And then, I told him what I thought when I picked the location, and where I would put people in the scene." Fassbinder would then come up with his own idea that he liked better based on Ballhaus' suggestion. This would provoke Ballhaus to come up with even better ideas the next day on the set, and the process would start all over again.

Sometimes it improves the work: "It became kind of a game—he always wanted to be better because he was very competitive, but I got better too," says Ballhaus, laughing. "We extended our game to be more and more sophisticated about the shots and the blocking."

> "When people go to the movies, they should not say, 'OK, this is a Michael Ballhaus film.' That would be wrong, in my view."

it works. But with something like **Goodfellas**, you have more freedom with lights—you can have more darkness, you can have more shadows, you can use different lenses. With **Goodfellas**, it doesn't really matter if you use a wide lens for a face that you normally would do with a long lens. It has to do with the story that you're telling—every movie that I do should look different to the other ones. When people go to the movies, they should not say, "OK, this is a Michael Ballhaus film." That would be wrong, in my view.

Goodfellas' famous tracking shot from the street into the Copacabana, was shot eight times or so. It was something that you had to be well prepared for. I had a very good Steadicam operator, and it was a hard scene to get, but we were so well planned and choreographed that wherever the problems were, we could solve them. That's one of my favorite shots, but not because of the technical aspects—I think it's just a fantastic idea because it's a shot that tells a story without dialogue. Ray Liotta's character cannot go to this girl and say, "Look, I'm a great guy, and I do this and that." Instead, he just walks in there, and the guys are really nice to him, and he gets the best table. And this girl is stunned—she is fascinated by him. This is the great thing about this scene: Yes, it's a long shot and it's a complicated shot, but the content—the storytelling of this shot—that is the real secret.

BRAM STOKER'S DRACULA

(01–02) Michael Ballhaus worked with the director Francis Ford Coppola on **Bram Stoker's Dracula**. Being filmed in the days of relatively simply technology, the special effects had to be imaginatively improvised. One scene which caused problems was the one in which Keanu Reeves had to be pulled into a room by Dracula. To create the illusion of gliding they built a seesaw with Keanu on one end and a weight on the other, so he could be lifted up. But Coppola also wanted to see Dracula extending his arm and pulling him in. The problem was solved by Pat Daily, their key grip, who suggested that they move the bench on which Dracula sits and put it on a dolly or a track.

GANGS OF NEW YORK

(01–06) Ballhaus was full of praise for the film's production designer Dante Ferretti. "When we arrived in Rome, five street sets were already finished, including a harbor with two maneuverable ships—every square foot was lovingly finished. We were able to shoot just as if we were on location, looking in all directions, even though we were on a studio lot."

To exploit the set's full potential Ballhaus used a lot of Steadicam. "We also used a lot of so-called Cable Cam, a construction where the camera is rigged to a cable spanning across the set. It enabled us to go from close to wide shot, all the while keeping the lens trained on a mid-nineteenth-century New York."

Ballhaus was unsure initially about working with the young superstar Leonardo DiCaprio, but he was pleasantly surprised. "He has this incredible sensitivity for the camera. He knows exactly where his light is."

The 360-degree track shot

For Rainer Werner Fassbinder's 1974 German TV movie **Martha**, Michael Ballhaus created what is believed to be cinema's first 360-degree tracking shot during an early scene in which Margit Carstensen and Karlheinz Böhm's characters share a brief first encounter that suggests an instant romantic spark.

Creating something memorable: According to Ballhaus, the pioneering shot happened almost by accident. "We came on the set," he recalls, "and Fassbinder said, 'I want the audience to know that with these two people, something will happen. What can we do to make it special so that it's not a regular shot?'" Ballhaus proposed tracking around the characters in a half-circle, which prompted Fassbinder to ask, "Why not all the way around?"

Best with level ground: This posed challenges, though: The ground they were shooting on wasn't level, and the shot would require the actors to step over the camera track. "When you watch the movie carefully, you can see that the lead actor does step over the track," Ballhaus says, laughing. "You can see he's lifting his leg."

Restrictions with the lighting: Nevertheless, the 360 tracking shot was born. "I hadn't seen anything like that before," he says. "For a cinematographer, it's hard to do a 360 because you can see everything—you cannot put any lights or anything up. Plus, the actors were turning too—the camera was not only tracking around them. But it created a shot that you would remember." The 360-degree track became Ballhaus's signature shot. **(01–02) The Age of Innocence**. Ballhaus' signature track (above) the fast-moving shot from the film (below).

James Wong Howe

James Wong Howe was born just shortly after moviemaking itself was. Few cinematographers did more to illustrate how the burgeoning art form could suggest mood and tone better than the man the industry nicknamed "Low-Key Howe" because of his brilliant use of low-light photography.

Born in 1899 in China under the name Wong Tung Jim, Howe moved with his family to a small town in Washington five years later. As a teenager, he wanted to pursue aviation, but instead he found himself working for director Cecil B. DeMille in Los Angeles, first as the kid who kept the camera department clean and then as the on-set clapper. Soon, he was a director of photography on silent films, but when motion pictures evolved to embrace sound, Howe, like many other technicians of the time, had to prove he could adapt to the new technology. He did just that, developing the use of deep-focus photography for the 1931 comedy **Transatlantic**,

"It's very easy, you know, to buy a light meter, but there's one thing that meter will not tell you, and that's whether you have the right mood or not. That you'll have to decide for yourself."

a full ten years before Gregg Toland brought the technique to its apex with **Citizen Kane**.

But Howe's innovations didn't end there. For director Robert Rossen's shattering 1947 boxing drama **Body and Soul**, Howe shot the fight scenes with a handheld camera while wearing roller skates, which gave the boxing matches a fluid, intimate urgency that had previously never seemed possible, inspiring director Martin Scorsese's **Raging Bull** (1980). His expertise with black-and-white photography continued with 1957's **Sweet Smell of Success**, which made the world of New York City nightlife seem as sexy and dangerous as anything seen in *film noir*.

01 James Wong Howe

Not that Howe wasn't equally adept with color: indeed, his Technicolor work on the 1955 romantic drama **Picnic** is as ravishing as the passion between the film's lovers, played by William Holden and Kim Novak. But Howe didn't believe color was automatically superior. "Color is very lavish, and I think if you find the right subject for it and put the people in there, it can be very good," he said in 1973. "But I don't think it's good to use color for color's sake. I think many color films should actually be made in black and white."

Nominated for ten Oscars and winning two, for 1955's **The Rose Tattoo** and 1963's **Hud**, Howe became renowned for using very little light to shoot his pictures. He credited his approach, in part, to coming of age as a cinematographer in an era when light meters weren't readily available. "We had to judge the exposure by looking through the camera," he explained, "either through the ground glass or sometimes through a piece of film." The unexpected benefit, he explained, was that "you can learn exposure if you observe light, which is the most important thing in photography." For Howe, mood was crucial. "It's very easy, you

know, to buy a light meter," he said. "But there's one thing that meter will not tell you, and that's whether you have the right mood or not. That you'll have to decide for yourself."

Above and beyond his cinematic achievements, Howe was also one of the first minorities to make an impact in the American film industry, even more remarkable considering that animosity toward Asians during World War II was so high that Japanese-Americans were being put into internment camps. And yet none of the bigotry surrounding Howe kept him from capturing the majesty of the world in his photography. After his death in 1976, his wife Sanora summed up his legacy as well as anyone ever has. "My husband loved his work," she wrote. "He was critical of poor quality in any area of film, but quick to see and appreciate the good. If the story allowed, his style was poetic realism, for he was a poet of the camera. This was a part of his nature, his impulse toward the beautiful, but it did not prevent his flexibility in dealing with all aspects of reality."

Ed Lachman

"Images shouldn't be only a pleasing pictorial aesthetic but a projection of the emotions that the characters discover in themselves."

Ed Lachman is a cinematographer whose work is both cerebral and inspired. Comfortable working with both European and American filmmakers, Lachman was born in Morristown, New Jersey, but made his name working for some of the major figures in the New German Cinema movement of the 1970s, including Werner Herzog, Wim Wenders, and Volker Schlondorff. In the 1980s, he moved between documentaries and feature films, notably **True Stories** (David Byrne, 1986), and **Less Than Zero** (Marek Kanievska, 1987). Soon after, he worked with writer–director Paul Schrader on **Light Sleeper** (1992), a thematic continuation of the filmmaker's "Man in a Room" series, which was preceded by **Taxi Driver** (1976) and **American Gigolo** (1980). When director Steven Soderbergh sought a stripped-down aesthetic for **The Limey** (1999) and **Erin Brockovich** (2000), he turned to Lachman as his DP, who provided a gritty, natural realism. But it's Lachman's work with Todd Haynes that has garnered the cinematographer his most accolades, first on the romantic melodrama **Far From Heaven** (2002), and then on the experimental Bob Dylan narrative **I'm Not There** (2007), and the HBO mini-series **Mildred Pierce** (2011). In between, he has worked with several of American independent cinema's most adventurous auteurs, including Sofia Coppola (**The Virgin Suicides**, 1999), Todd Solondz (**Life During Wartime**, 2009), and Robert Altman (**A Prairie Home Companion**, 2006). At the same time, he remains connected to world cinema and is one of the cinematographers of Austrian director Ulrich Seidl's **Import/Export** (2007), which was in competition at Cannes, and his latest film, **Paradise** (2011). Lachman has a video installation and photos in the permanent collection of the Whitney Museum of Art, New York, and shows photos and films in museums and galleries throughout the world.

Ed Lachman

"My father owned a small movie theater as a film exhibitor while representing a French company in North America that produced light sources for movie projectors, called art carbons, for commercial cinemas. So I was around film my whole life, but I didn't take it very seriously. My father also was an amateur photographer, but as a child I shied away and abhorred cameras—I always had this idea or concept, like Eastern thought, that a photographic image could steal your soul.

When I was in art school I studied art history and painting—I wanted to be a painter. But I took a survey course at Harvard—an appreciation of film history from Dwight Macdonald and Italian cinema from Gideon Bachmann—and that's when it clicked. I was always interested in Dadaism and the found image in art, so the fact that you could pick up the camera and find an image and create a story connected with me.

I also saw **Umberto D** (1952), an Italian neorealist film by Vittorio De Sica, in which the director relied heavily on the image rather than the words to tell the story. He constructed the story through images to create the emotional context and thematics for the viewer. I realized that those images don't just get up there on the screen—they're there for a reason. The idea of constructing images to tell stories—that's what really fascinated me.

So, then I got interested in how to create images for films. I thought, "Well, the best way to learn about making films is to make and shoot my own films." They were kind of imagistic, towards documentary—they were more like portraits of individuals that I met. I thought about how painters would always come from a certain personal, social, and political position about why they painted and how they painted. So I thought you could do that in a film—that you could come from a certain idea about the image rather than just trying to make an image aesthetically beautiful. I guess people liked the way my films looked and asked me to shoot their films. Because filmmaking is so expensive I thought I would learn how to make films through working →

01–02 Erin Brockovich

Creating a retro feel

(01–02) During Ed Lachman's initial conversations with director Sofia Coppola about making **The Virgin Suicides**, she mentioned being inspired by **Badlands**. "She liked the way that movie had a certain '70s feeling," Lachman explains.

Use a low-contrast Kodak film: "So I began to shoot tests with different film stocks and found a low-contrast Kodak stock, 5277, that I had never used before. It was softer, muted, and had noticeable grain to it. I thought it would help create a forlorn nostalgia in the mood of the story. I discovered the stock was being discontinued and had to find all that was left of it in Canada and the US to be able to use it. The film's pastel quality and the way it rendered colors also helped to create the images of fantasy and desire of the adolescents, like the melancholy longing of the novel."

on other people's projects. And that's what I did, but I ended up being a cameraman while trying to make my own films.

Werner Herzog gave me my first real break. I met him in Berlin—I was in school in France, and his first feature film, **Signs of Life** (1968) was screened at the Berlin Film Festival. We became friends, and I thought his film was austere, poetic and quite remarkable. Germany at the time in the '70s was finally reemerging culturally with the rest of the world through its films. Werner, without looking at a foot of film, said, "I'd like you to work with me on my next film," and that became **La Soufrière**, a documentary in Guadalupe about a small group of inhabitants who were poor and resisted "God and country," as Werner said, that refused to be evacuated from the island in spite of the imminent volcanic eruption. So, we went to

Guadalupe and made this film—thank God the volcano didn't erupt. We were on the volcano, with billowing sulfuric smoke all around us, looking for these souls who resisted being saved, and I naively asked, "What will happen if the volcano erupts? What will we do?" Werner looked straight at me and said, "We'll be skyborne."

I've also always been interested in the use of color to create emotions rather than just a pictorial representation and how different light sources—tungsten, florescent, sodium, or mercury vapor—mixed or individually create a mood through the different color temperatures they portray on film. I looked at color photography from Joel Meyerowitz, or William Eggleston, or Len Jenshel, or the photographers that were exploring new work in the '70s—they were using

FAR FROM HEAVEN

(01–05) "**Far From Heaven** created a Douglas Sirk world of his 1950s' Hollywood melodramas. Sirk was one of the last filmmakers who fled from Nazi Germany before the war. His roots were in German theater, and he used Brechtian techniques of gesture, light, and color to create a world of artifice. He felt that creating this expressionistic world allowed the audience to connect to their emotions. Sirk developed a theatrical visual style that conveyed his political and social criticism of the status quo of America's social, racial, and sexual mores. **Far From Heaven** explored the idea of repression through beauty. The surface beauty of the characters' world becomes its betrayal. Ironically, they are seduced by what keeps them from their desire. The Julianne Moore character, Cathy, is always moving through her picture-perfect world, but somehow never finding the emotional stability of what middle-class life is supposed to be."

> "In my work, I think each film has its own methodology, language, and style because of what it evolves out of."

6x9 and 8x10 larger-format cameras but shooting on locations with natural light, mixing color temperatures. Also, the early color films of Wim Wenders that Robby Müller shot—I always responded to the way they used color shifts from different sources. Tungsten, florescent, daylight, sodium vapor—I always felt that gave a certain emotional feeling to the locations and the characters. It created a way of looking into the interior world from the outside.

I've always played with color gels and color temperature, I guess since **Desperately Seeking Susan** (1985), as an expressionistic tool. For **The Virgin Suicides**, the idea for me was how you create these two different worlds: the feminine adolescent world that's always unobtainable and a mystery to the male adolescent world. So I created a color palette to make the world of the girls in magentas and blues seem distant. They were enclosed and entrapped in their house, so the light from the curtained windows was always cool. I wanted to make them feel like they were imprisoned in their own childlike world. The boys were always on the outside looking in—in neutral color temperatures to a summery warm one outside—to create a feeling of the boys being voyeurs of what they didn't understand in their desires.

In my work, I think each film has its own methodology, language and style because of what it evolves out of. With **I'm Not There**, we made a film as an essay/poem on the cultural myths and politics that transformed Bob Dylan and his reaction to it. Through the '60s and '70s cinema and popular culture, we approached the script for **I'm Not There** as an assemblage of →

Bob Dylan inhabiting different creative personas of himself and referencing his influences. Todd Haynes' script approached Dylan by different visual languages and textures for the varied worlds of each of his six different characters portraying aspects of Dylan's life, just like an artist reinventing himself with his music, pushing himself artistically and shedding his persona with each new album. We visually referenced the '60s and '70s period of filmmaking from Europe's French New Wave—specifically early Godard, for his polemic frames that felt random with available naturalistic lighting imbued with his sexual politics—to Italy of early Antonioni and Fellini, breaking away from the postwar neorealism to the more personal and subjective style of the modern Italian 8½.

We also drew from the experimentation in '70s Hollywood filmmaking, such as the counterculture antihero westerns like George Roy Hill's **Butch Cassidy and the Sundance Kid**, which was photographed by Conrad Hall, Robert

Altman's **McCabe and Mrs. Miller**, which was photographed by Vilmos Zsigmond, and Sam Peckinpah's **Pat Garrett and Billy the Kid**, which was photographed by John Coquillon. These cameramen were coming out of commercials, experimenting with the use of zooms and longer lenses with strong backlight and flares, and chocolate and coral filters. These all seemed to be out of date now, but we recreated this effect for the section of Richard Gere playing the western outlaw on the run.

What is the challenge of cinematography? What will tell the poetic or psychological truth of an image in our story? Images shouldn't be only a pleasing pictorial aesthetic, but a projection of the emotions that the characters discover in themselves. Literature can enter the interior world of the character, but it's much more difficult in writing to show where you are—authors spend paragraphs and pages illustrating place. In film, you can show the exterior world with one shot, but

THE LIMEY

(01–03) "**The Limey** was a stylistic homage to the experimental fractured-time and urban nightmare of John Boorman's '60s LA noir classic **Point Blank** and the early-'70s **Get Carter**, a nihilistic neo-noir of Mike Hodges' that renders the world of a loner seeking revenge like Terence Stamp in **The Limey**." Ed Lachman and director Steven Soderbergh shot with available light, practicals, and mixed color temperatures and improvised with two cameras. "Steven was on one of the cameras, and it became very liberating for him, directly connecting to the image through the viewfinder and in a sense being the first audience for the actors. From that film on, he became his own cameraman," Lachman recalls, adding with a laugh, "he told me he was becoming bored with just directing."

"No take is ever the same—the performance, the rhythm of the camera, or where the actors position themselves in the light."

it's much more difficult to enter the interior world of a character with a camera. That's what I'm always trying to explore with a director: how you enter the interior world of the character and his emotions. Images are metaphors to uncover something not hidden on the surface that create an emotional landscape for your characters and story.

With **Erin Brockovich**, Steven Soderbergh's approach was, "How do you create an honest, raw portrayal of a working-class mom with a Hollywood star like Julia Roberts?" We set our visual limitations as if we were making a lower-budget, independent film. Ninety percent of the film was shot on actual locations where the story took place, with the natural light we would find on location or on set. Film stocks today have so much exposure latitude that when we shot all the daytime car shots, even in the desert, we used the available sunlight without using any lights to balance the interior of the car with the exterior. To create the feeling of realism or a documentary sense of the world, we didn't rely on the use of a handheld camera to create an emotional realism as if the audience is experiencing the performance in real time. I think that device has been overused and can lose its effectiveness, and for some filmmakers it relinquishes their responsibility to know how to tell the story effectively with the camera. When it's done well, with a sense of discovery, rhythm and poetics, as in Wong Kar-wai's **In the Mood for Love**, it can be brilliant. Or the Austrian cinematographer Wolfgang Thaler, who I worked with on two Ulrich Seidl films, **Import/Export** and **Paradise**, who finds an emotional rhythm with the actors in the storytelling, either on his shoulder or on the tripod. I approached **The Limey**, **Erin Brockovich**, and **A Prairie Home Companion** as I did my own film **Ken Park**, from a more Eastern European approach. The camera documents the performance in real time on a tripod or dolly moving with the performance, and I construct one shot as an extension of time to another with extended takes, editing in camera, and following the characters' actions and portraying their point of view in the storytelling.

When I research a period for a film, I might not only look at other films of that time, but also writers, music and painters or whatever visual cues the script gives me. I go to directors when I've read a script and present them with a kind of visual notebook. Some directors embrace that—even if it isn't their ideas, at least it starts a forum for discussion. So you have to find your footing with the director for how you create that language, because for me the language of cinema is images. The images are the subtext for the psychological world that you create for the characters.

An image is also an extension of your own point of view. In a photograph by, let's say, Robert Frank or William Eggleston, you're seeing a poetic and subjective viewpoint of that image. Everybody can look at that same image and see it in different ways. That's what separates one artist from another: what their experience is with that image. For me, images are about experiencing something with your camera. It's the immediacy of that experience that you're capturing, even in the narrative form. No take is ever the same—the performance, the rhythm of the camera, or where the actors position themselves in the light.

Robert Altman wanted that immediacy to allow the audience to feel that they're participating and discovering something happening before their eyes. Shooting **A Prairie Home Companion** was like improvisational jazz. He was very much into improvisation—with the performances, and with what the camera did. He would just set up multiple cameras on a track, sometimes facing each other in their movement, and used the camera as a performance with the actors. The problem for the cameraman is where you place your light with multiple cameras, but he would always laugh and say, "That's your problem." He knew very well what the effect was that he wanted, and he didn't want to be restricted by how he told the story—he wanted to create this feeling of discovery and improvisation with the camera, as in jazz. →

"I really think once you can start thinking about ideas in images, then you're not trying to create just visually pleasing images that never transcend their own clichés."

I've worked with Wim Wenders, Godard, Bertolucci and Seidl, and they all have their own cinematic language. So you kind of plug into that language and put your own input into it, but I'm working within their language. That's the way it was with Altman—I knew that the dictates of him shooting two or three cameras and moving the camera all the time would create its own aesthetic. When I once worked with Godard, he told me to keep everybody in the middle of the frame, and I thought, "Hmm, that's gonna be weird for composition." Later when I looked at the footage, the compositions were really interesting—it created its own style. Images for Godard are always about the idea behind the image rather than just some aesthetic. I really think once you can start thinking about ideas in images, then you're not trying to create just visually pleasing images that never transcend their own clichés.

Film versus digital? Well, Todd Haynes and myself decided to shoot **Mildred Pierce** on film using Super 16 to maintain a film look. I know everyone is interested in digital formats and the advances that digital cameras are making today. I have shot two films with digital cameras, **A Prairie Home Companion** and **Life During Wartime**, but for me, the tests I've done show that film still has a greater exposure latitude and the way it renders color is different, whether in color temperature or using gels. In film emulsion, the grain structure or silver halide crystals are in a random pattern in the three color layers—red, green and blue—which creates the film's look and texture. In film, depth between the layers—even though they're microscopic—when exposed to light present a sense of depth in light and shadow and color separation, like an etching. The problem is, on a digital chip everything is rendered on one plain in a pixel-fixed location, and it lacks depth and separation to my eye. It might be my age—I grew up seeing photographic images exposed on film, but someone younger than myself that grew up on digital images may prefer seeing digital. There seems to be more interest and acceptance in creating digital imagery today, but for me right now as a way of creating the image, film still has more versatility and sensitivity. The film's marriage with the digital world—color correcting your film in a digital intermediate or digitally projecting the final film—seems like the best of both worlds. I found it definitely more expensive and time-consuming to create digital images that come closest to film. I always find it interesting that they always talk about how digital media should be like film, but I never hear talk about how film should be more like digital.

After all this time, I still respond to the found image—I like how one sees reality and then interprets it. Even on films like **Far From Heaven** and **Mildred Pierce**, I still base that in some reality to create the illusion. Well, then, that's an interesting point: If films are the illusion of reality, what is reality but still our illusion? So once you realize that you can deal with reality as the illusion, you can create your illusion as a reality.

MILDRED PIERCE

(01–04) Director Todd Haynes and Lachman decided to forgo the consciously stylized dramatic studio look of the classic '30s and '40s noir lighting. Instead, they designed a style that echoed neo-noir films of the '70s, which found a distance in their expressionistic naturalism. "We also looked at the work of Saul Leiter. Leiter was a street still photographer who worked more like a painter. He used found objects, textures, and reflections as the content for his images. For **Mildred Pierce** we tried to create a certain distance to her, as if she is being observed. The images of Mildred are seen through objects, reflections in mirrors, and through bevel-glassed doors, fragmenting her world, and creating a prismed dislocation for her. The images become not only a representational view of the world but a psychological one." As for the color palette, Haynes and Lachman looked at the early color still photography of the '30s,

including photographers commissioned by the Farm Security Administration that documented not only the Dust Bowl during The Depression, but also images of cities like Los Angeles. "The early color film of this time was more limited, and the saturation and contrast were very different to today's full-range color negatives. We did everything possible to capture this and the reality of people trying to survive, even in their middle-class privilege, during The Depression. We tried to recreate LA's harsh sunlight and the atmosphere of pollution and grittiness in muted saturated colors of magentas, greens and yellows."

Rodrigo Prieto

"I don't think 'good' photography is always 'beautiful' photography...I think it's not about that—images should just be what moves you and what will support the story."

Born in Mexico City, Rodrigo Prieto started off making short films and commercials for more than a decade before coming to the world's attention with his daring work on **Amores Perros** (2000), his first feature with director Alejandro González Iñárritu. His partnership with Iñárritu continues to this day, as they have worked together on **21 Grams** (2003), **Babel** (2006) and **Biutiful** (2010). Their films are known for their unconventional narratives, often jumbling the chronology of events or telling separate (but sometimes interrelated) storylines. In addition, Prieto's work with Iñárritu has focused on handheld camera, which gives their urgent tales a gritty, raw quality. Prieto has also collaborated with Spike Lee on **25th Hour** (2002), Curtis Hanson on **8 Mile** (2002) and Pedro Almodóvar on **Broken Embraces** (2009). He received an Oscar nomination for Ang Lee's **Brokeback Mountain** (2005)—and he would reunite with Lee on a very different love story in 2007, the Shanghai-set period thriller **Lust, Caution**. Quite comfortable with both the boldness of Iñárritu and the simplicity of Lee, Prieto has also worked with Oliver Stone for his opulent historical epic **Alexander** (2004) and his **Wall Street** sequel **Wall Street: Money Never Sleeps** (2010).

Rodrigo Prieto

" My introduction to filmmaking was stop-motion. I was a big fan of Ray Harryhausen, and when I was around 11 years old I used to make these plasticine monsters with my older brother Antonio. But then we learned that we could make these monsters come alive through stop-motion. My father had an 8mm Bell & Howell camera, and we learned how to expose and how to design the movements. That changed my life forever. But I still wasn't seriously considering a career in film, because I was in Mexico and in my family there wasn't really anyone who was working in the film business. I didn't have a concept that that was possible—I just enjoyed doing these little science-fiction movies. Later, I discovered special effects, and then we evolved to Super 8 and sound and editing and rewinding the film. We were doing scratches on the film to create lasers and explosions and stuff like that. That's how we would play.

When I went to film school in Mexico City, it was simply an opportunity to keep playing, to keep doing my little movies. But then that school closed, so I started working in a still photography studio—I did the lab and the prints and carried equipment. I worked for Nadine Markova, a still photographer—she was my mentor. By the end of the year that I spent working with her, she shot a movie as a director of photography—it was called **Welcome Maria**, which was done here in LA She brought me along—I was the apprentice of the camera crew, and that's when I fell in love with cinematography. I remember walking into the camera truck and smelling the gear and smelling the oil of the camera—I'll never forget that. I said, "This is it."

I attended another film school and I knew that I wanted to be a cinematographer, although I was still interested in directing. In the first year of film school, I had so much fun shooting the movies of other directors. I directed my own film, which I enjoyed, but I really enjoyed the craft and the

LUST, CAUTION

(01–03) The romantic drama **Lust, Caution** presented logistical problems because of its period setting. "Ang Lee is really a stickler for authenticity," Rodrigo Prieto says. "We were filming in modern Hong Kong, which is really modern—and Shanghai, for that matter. Making them look like they were in the '30s was really complex." To accurately capture the era required "a combination of visual effects and sometimes choosing the right angles and hiding things with art department pieces."

01

energy of shooting. Lighting, preparing the camera—that was very exciting to me. And I remember that the students that were focusing on directing were very serious, but with cinematography you got to play—no one was worrying about what you did or didn't do. I found that it was more exciting and playful, and I was lucky because back then there weren't that many students who wanted to be cinematographers. In fact, it was only two of us out of 12, so we got to shoot a lot. Those films that I shot in film school were seen by producers and directors, and that's how I started getting my first jobs.

I find that it really is not that different right now to how it was in film school. Obviously, there's different equipment, different budgets—certainly different budgets—but the level of responsibility felt the same in film school. It was life or death—if the movie you were doing for your friend came out well or was underexposed, it was always life or death. So that's one thing I always say to students: "Enjoy film school. And keep doing it." You know, it's not like film school is to prepare you for the day you'll "make it"—I think it's part of the same process. In fact, when you're working you're still in film school—every day I'm learning. It's not that much different, except now my fellow cinematographers are my teachers.

When I read a script for the first time, it's just a story. I try not to even think about photography, although it's sort of inevitable that I will, because in life I'm always looking at the light around me. But it's only on the second read that I start imagining things: "How could I represent this visually?" Then after that, I look for images. I have a collection of photography books, but typically I'll go to a photography bookshop and just sort of let myself feel the ideas, and look at books and books and books. Lots of times as I'm looking at images, I'm not quite conscious of what it is about an image that startles me. But sometimes I'll →

Widescreen vs 1:85

Understand the visual elements of the story:
"One of my first conversations with Ang Lee about **Brokeback Mountain (01–04)** was about the aspect ratio of the movie," Prieto says. "Your first tendency would be, 'Let's shoot this widescreen because of the vistas.' But when we started talking about it, we realized that it was about a mountain first of all, which is vertical. And it was about the body language of these characters—it's just basically the two of them. So we thought we could fit these two characters very well within the 1:85 aspect ratio. The composition of the mountain and the sky for us made more sense in 1:85—we knew that was an important visual element of the location but also the story. We certainly needed to feel the environment these characters are in."

Get a different feel for interior and exterior locations: To help separate the cowboys' experience on **Brokeback Mountain** from their lives at home, Prieto shot the mountains with a 50 ASA stock: "It was pristine and clean and basically grainless. For the rest of the story, I used 500 ASA and 250 ASA so it's a little bit more grainy. I didn't push anything—it's very subtle, but it is grainier. I just wanted to feel like you could breathe the crispness of mountain air."

> **"As a cinematographer, I've learned to be very flexible in that regard and understand that every director has a different way of approaching a film."**

look at an image and think, "Oh yeah, that color can work for such-and-such scene." Then I make color photocopies and put a thing together and present it to the director. Also, before I talk to a director, I do my own shot list. Then I present these ideas to the director, and we take it from there. Sometimes, the director has a completely different idea, and sometimes from our two sets of ideas we come up with a hybrid. Maybe we'll end up going with the director's idea. But for me, bringing to the table ideas of how to shoot a scene is a good starting point to design the look and feel of a film with the director.

With Alejandro González Iñárritu, we do shot lists extensively. We sit down and I do this process, and he does his own, and then we compare notes. All the movies we've done are quite designed, actually—even though the movies seem improvised because of the handheld camera. It seems like we're just capturing whatever's happening, and that's the intention, but it's always really planned out, particularly in terms of transitions and how a scene will start editorially or how it will end, going into a different scene. We've done several movies where the structure was complex, so beforehand we know how it's going to come together. We really design how we come out of a scene and maybe go into another scene of a different story in a way that we felt would be a good cut. So that's why we do such extensive shot lists.

Other directors, like Ang Lee, don't do a shot list. His way of approaching it is he sees a rehearsal with the actors on that day, and I usually think of what directions we could potentially shoot, and sometimes maybe he'll have an idea of a certain way of shooting that we've discussed beforehand. But nothing is written. He's super-specific in terms of how he wants the framing, the camera position, the lens, so he will actually ask for, say, a 32mm lens. He'll have the key grip mark the floor and measure the shot. For me, that was totally different—I was not used to that. But that's his way, and I learned to work with him like that. He certainly has an incredible eye, so everything he was asking for just made perfect sense—it was great. Of the directors I have worked with, he is probably the most specific—other directors will talk about, say, focal lengths or will be more generic about lenses, but Ang Lee is super-precise. For him, there's a difference between a 27 and a 25; it has to be a 27—that's how he envisions it. As a cinematographer, I've learned to be very flexible in that regard and understand that every director has a different way of approaching a film. And I find that by learning to work in any style, I grow as a filmmaker.

Now with Oliver Stone, he's not only really open to ideas, but he expects his team to propose concepts. It's really exciting working with him that way because—while he certainly has his own ideas as well—he expects you to propose, like, "How about we do this scene →

04

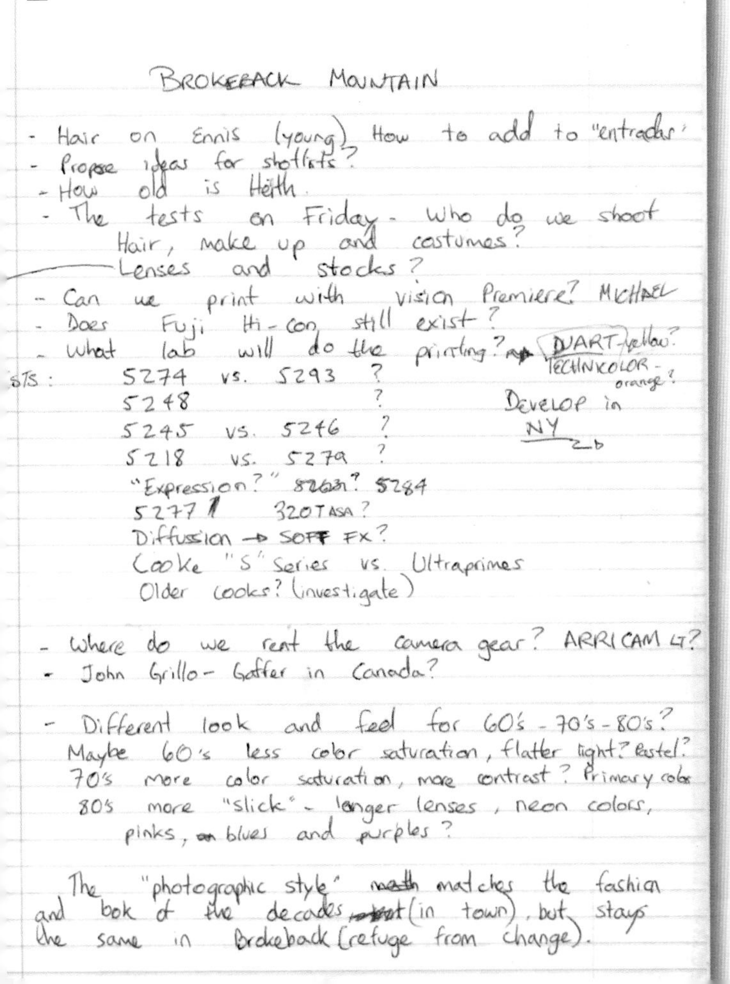
BROKEBACK MOUNTAIN

- Hair on Ennis (young). How to add to "entradas"
- Propose ideas for shotlists?
- How old is Heith
- The tests on Friday - Who do we shoot
  Hair, make up and costumes?
  Lenses and stocks?
- Can we print with vision Premiere? MICHAEL
- Does Fuji Hi-con still exist?
- What lab will do the printing? DUART - yellow? TECHNICOLOR - orange?
  DEVELOP in NY

STS: 5274 vs. 5293 ?
5248 ?
5245 vs. 5246 ?
5218 vs. 5279 ?
"Expression?" 8263? 5284
5277 320T ASA?
Diffusion → SOFT FX?
Cooke "S" Series vs. Ultraprimes
Older cooks? (investigate)

- Where do we rent the camera gear? ARRICAM 4?
- John Grillo - Gaffer in Canada?

- Different look and feel for 60's - 70's - 80's?
  Maybe 60's less color saturation, flatter light? Pastel?
  70's more color saturation, more contrast? Primary colors
  80's more "slick" - longer lenses, neon colors, pinks, blues and purples?

The "photographic style" matches the fashion and look of the decades (in town), but stays the same in Brokeback (refuge from change).

> **"I like to operate the camera because I connect to the story and to the actors, and I find that really exciting and just a good experience for me."**

like this?" Each department proposes where they want to take something, and then the idea is bounced back and forth. Ang Lee's films are so subtle, whereas with Oliver everything has to be big. So I get to play in a big way with Oliver, and with Ang Lee it's about designing very little—the difference between 200 ASA and 400 ASA. With Ang Lee, I get to play in a much more subtle way, and I like that too—it's like rock 'n' roll versus a string quartet. As a cinematographer, that's an opportunity I enjoy a lot, working with people who have such diverse approaches and energies and you get to be both.

I operate the camera practically every time. For me it is very important to feel the energy of the actors. I learned to do cinematography like that in Mexico, and so it just became my natural way of working where I'm at the same time working the camera, designing the lighting,

rehearsing the moves, and understanding the edges of the frame and what's not in frame. It's a process that I can't separate, so I do it simultaneously. But more than that, it's like—I don't do music, but if I would compose music and give it to someone to perform, it's fine, but for me playing the instrument is like operating the camera. It's really feeling it—you're the first one to see the performance of an actor. You get the biggest impact that anybody will ever have—you're right there, feeling the energy, and it's focused into this lens, which, optically, is your eye. So, it's just emotional. I like to operate the camera because I connect to the story and to the actors, and I find that really exciting and just a good experience for me.

Alejandro likes the spontaneous feeling of handheld and the participation of the camera in a scene. It somehow makes the audience feel

8 MILE

(01–03) For this film the lighting and color scheme were influenced by a mural by the artist Diego Rivera of the US auto industry that hangs in the Detroit Institute of Arts. "The coloration of this mural is very cyan—bluish cyan—with shades of green, I guess because of the lighting of these places. So when I started shooting tests for **8 Mile**, I tested all these florescent fixtures uncorrected—to get that cyan hue."

01

NOTES AND SHOTLISTS

Sc. 1: Night Int. Bathroom

Start on reflection on mirror. We discover it's a reflection when Jimmy enters frame in the foreground? Pull back from reflection to find him and follow him in reality. vs.
several tight shots of action → confusion frantic? - Also: Jim in foreground, door in background?
Idea: At some point have Jimmy look directly at the camera (his reflection?) Dirty glass (mirror") in foreground. Maybe tilt up from his hands in wash basin after puking to him looking at himself.

- Overhead shot of him puking in stall

Sc. 2-3:
① Start "objective" pan with him leaving the bathroom, follow behind him until the big bad dude stops him (over Jimmy's shoulder). Future enters frame.
② C.U. of Jimmy over BBD's shoulder.

③ "Backstage" Two shot of Jimmy + Future camera pulls back with them; the door to the backstage behind them. Jimmy leaves, Future behind him.

BROKEN EMBRACES

(04–07) Prieto stresses the importance of serving the vision of the director first and foremost, as demonstrated by his work on Pedro Almodóvar's **Broken Embraces**. "It's a Pedro Almodóvar movie—it looks like a Pedro Almodóvar movie," he says. "I like being able to understand a director's perspective and to be able to support him. I think, 'OK, what is it that makes you tick? Why do you see something this way?' I want to explore that and see what it is about a director that makes him unique. I don't want to break that."

like they really literally are a character or a participant. Before we did movies together, we did many, many commercials that were not handheld at all. Alejandro's energy is really intense, and I think the handheld camera really translates that well visually—the texture of it just matches Alejandro's energy. Another director might say, "Move the camera so it looks energetic," and that's frankly something that I do not like. I try to have the camera move if the scene's energy makes it move. But to artificially say, "Let's make it look handheld…" I actually try to be as stable as possible with the camera.

But of course, sometimes you're running with the camera, so there's nothing you can do. In **Biutiful**, when the police are chasing the street vendors, that was all me—oh my God, I could have died doing that, literally. I had talked a lot with my key grip and Alejandro about how to shoot that with the camera traveling backward and with someone running at full speed. I knew that I simply couldn't keep up, and it was certainly dangerous, you know, to run backward like that. So I tested different methods, and we settled on this little golf cart. We shot a few takes with the actors running past, and Alejandro didn't like it—he said, "No, it looks too perfect." I was like, "Come on, the camera was bouncing all →

21 GRAMS

(01–03) Beyond the physical demands of operating a camera, Prieto has also had to contend with the unexpected emotional repercussions. "I have had moments with the camera where I'm moved to tears," he admits, "and it's been sometimes hard to keep operating the camera effectively because the viewfinder's all teared up and I'm starting to actually physically move with my crying. It happened twice on **21 Grams** with Naomi Watts—she just touched something in me." He says he has learned to control his emotions better over time, but he remains very connected to the scenes he's shooting. "Especially in a movie when it's handheld, the rhythm of the camera is totally dictated by the rhythm of the actors. I try to kinda breathe with them with the camera. But it is physically exhausting—I don't think I'll be able to do it for many more years."

> "...it's traditionally considered part of a cinematographer's job to make the lead actors look beautiful—but I don't think that's necessarily the case."

over—what do you mean 'perfect?'" So finally, he said, "Just do one handheld." So I did a few takes and, of course, the actors catch up to me and I have to go faster, so I had someone behind me watching. On one take, I tripped on something and flew backwards, but the key grip caught me, thank God. Somehow I kept the camera from being destroyed, but, man, I was really scared. I mean, falling backwards like that at full speed… but Alejandro will do anything to get what he wants. Nothing gets in his way.

When I have to find a way to enhance the beauty of an actress, I do enjoy it. For example, with Penélope Cruz in **Broken Embraces**, I carefully studied her face to design the best lighting for her. We shot a lot of tests, lighting her like this and lighting her like that—it was important that the audience would fall in love with her like the characters do. But—and I may lose jobs by saying this—it's traditionally considered part of a cinematographer's job to make the lead actors look beautiful—but I don't think that's necessarily the case. I think that it is in certain movies, like **Broken Embraces** or **Lust, Caution**. But I think what's important is if it makes sense for the character. So in **Lust, Caution**, the main character played by Tang Wei had to be two different people in a way. She's pretending to be this sophisticated woman who seduces men, and she had to look gorgeous—so I lit her differently than when she was the ugly duckling in school. Or in **8 Mile**, Kim Basinger is beautiful, but I

> **"I just like to be moved, and if I can participate in moving people I find that really exciting."**

didn't light her to be gorgeous because it didn't fit this woman in a trailer park who has gone through what she has gone through. It has to be organic to the character—it's something that I'll discuss with the director, and we'll decide what is needed.

Likewise, I don't think "good" photography is always "beautiful" photography. Usually people think that—they'll talk about "good" cinematography and say, "It's so beautiful. Oh, those are beautiful images." But I don't think it's about that—images should just be what moves you and what will support the story.

I just like to be moved, and if I can participate in moving people I find that really exciting. So that's why I gravitate to scripts that are emotional and stirring. From that moment as a kid that I saw the reaction of my friends to the monsters that we made in stop-motion—seeing them blown away by suddenly seeing a monster their size projected on a sheet, and seeing that I could make them scream and laugh and run away and be delighted with a camera—I said, "This is what I want to do."

BIUTIFUL

(04–05) Depending on the intention of the particular scene in **Biutiful**, Prieto would use anamorphic or spherical lenses, which would affect depth of field and the image texture. In addition, he utilized C-series flare lenses precisely because they create extreme flare when they're pointed toward light sources. These different lenses allowed Prieto and director Alejandro González Iñárritu to map the evolution of Javier Bardem's character from a man desperate to maintain control to someone who accepts his fate.

Caleb Deschanel

"The closest that I can think of to what I do visually
is what a symphony does. It's really like music—it
has different movements."

A five-time Oscar nominee, Caleb Deschanel was part of a group of young American filmmakers who came of age during Hollywood's creative renaissance of the 1970s, inspired by the avant-garde work of French New Wave directors such as Jean-Luc Godard and François Truffaut. Going to the University of Southern California in 1967 to study film and then later to the American Film Institute, Deschanel befriended two film students at nearby UCLA: Francis Ford Coppola and Carroll Ballard. With Coppola executive producing and Ballard directing, Deschanel shot **The Black Stallion** (1979), one of cinema's greatest family films and which earned him a Best Cinematography award from the Los Angeles Film Critics Association. Deschanel's gorgeous, quietly observant shooting style—inspired in part by his earlier work shooting education films—was later incorporated into the muted comedy of **Being There** (Hal Ashby, 1979), the docu-drama realism of **The Right Stuff** (Philip Kaufman, 1983), and the mythic wonder of **The Natural** (Barry Levinson, 1984). He has shown an ability to work on both large-scale action movies, such as **National Treasure** (Jon Turteltaub, 2004), and intimate love stories such as **Message in a Bottle** (Luis Mandoki, 1999), but one of the consistent hallmarks of his work is an emphasis on stories with inspirational or humanistic themes. A director of both film and television, Deschanel won the ASC award for **The Patriot** (Roland Emmerich, 2000) and in 2010 was honored with the organization's Lifetime Achievement Award.

Caleb Deschanel

" When I was a child, I got a Brownie Hawkeye still camera—to be honest, I can't remember if I had asked for it or not. What I do remember is taking photographs, and then when I would get them back I would notice that some photographs were better than others. So it was from that point that I developed an eye: "Oh, I like this. I don't like that." I had a real sense of both composition and emotional content. I think that's the most important thing about what cinematographers do: We bring an emotional context from a visual point of view.

I went to Johns Hopkins as an undergraduate, and I started out doing some pre-med courses. In high school, my subjects were mathematics and science: physics, chemistry, biology. I really liked the sciences, and my dad was an engineer. I liked solving problems, which is a lot of what you do when you're shooting a movie: "We don't have the budget for that, so let's do it this way." It's constant problem-solving.

At Hopkins, I really got interested in the history of art. There was a professor teaching there named Phoebe Stanton, and I remember wandering into her class one day. She projected slides of great paintings and architecture, and I really loved it. I mean, I like sitting in a dark room looking at images.

I went to USC film school, and then to the AFI. I wanted to have an internship with a cinematographer. The AFI wanted me to have one with some old-style Hollywood cameraman, but the reason I got involved in film really had to do with the French New Wave and Raoul Coutard and Godard and Truffaut. I really liked their style— it was the antitheses of Hollywood moviemaking of big cranes and sweeping shots. I didn't particularly like the way Hollywood movies were lit because I felt there was an artificiality to them. Gordon Willis was just coming up—he'd shot **End of the Road** (1970) and **Loving** (1970), and I really liked his style of shooting. The AFI didn't →

THE NATURAL
(01–02) For every movie Deschanel shoots, such as **The Natural**, he takes a similar initial approach. "I like to take every scene in a movie, read it, understand it, and think about what's important," he says. "For instance, if there's a moment where a character needs to make a decision, you need to be close on them, but if there's just some exposition, you can be further back. If somebody is expressing something with body language, you can be back for a full shot. I'll think, 'OK, what size do I need to be here? How can I do this in one shot?' It may not be the way I'm going to shoot it, but I'd like to have an understanding that helps me know dramatically what's important in the scene."

03

THE RIGHT STUFF

(03–05) The Right Stuff tells the epic story of the early days of America's space program, and Deschanel sought to ground the story in reality. "I approached that movie in a sort of documentary fashion," he says. "It was important that you don't taint the reality with any kind of obvious mythology, because you need the audience to understanding that these guys were real." That included working with Gary Gutierrez, who supervised the film's special effects, to ensure that the flying sequences weren't too polished. "Director Phil Kaufman and I really wanted all the special effects to be kind of gritty. When we were shooting the plane scenes, we were shaking the camera and doing all this stuff that would happen if you were actually there." His vigorous shaking of the camera resulted in Deschanel accidentally giving his operator a black eye at one point.

04

05

want me to go to New York to intern for somebody who they didn't know about, but I just recognized in his style something that I thought was really great.

I observed him on a film called **The People Next Door** (1970), which he shot before **The Godfather** (1972). I charted all the lighting setups; I would read the f-stops with my light meter and make detailed notes. I was really obsessed—I would go to the lab with Gordie [Gordon Willis] and he would talk to me about what they had done, and how it was exposed. It was really a crash course in almost every aspect of making movies. It wasn't a particularly great movie, but for me it was wonderful because Gordie really took the time and told me a lot of what he was doing.

Because I had studied with Gordie, I had an idea from watching him about how to shoot features. I had not worked my way up, so I had not observed anyone on a big film before. But going into **The Black Stallion**, I felt that I was drawing more from my experience shooting documentaries and educational films. I had done this educational film, a documentary about a farm family in Iowa, and you're really just observing people—most of the time nothing happens. But I got to the point where I could read people, and I would just know: "That guy's gonna get up now, and he's gonna go over to the kitchen." You became a real observer and you develop an understanding of behavior. The style of **The Black Stallion** was very much derived from that sort of educational documentary approach where, basically, Carroll would set up situations: "OK, you've got to feed the horse" or "OK, now you've got to cut the horse loose." He set up these situations, and because both Carroll and I were so used to filming documentaries, we would watch and record it on film anticipating what would happen next.

Carroll is a very instinctive and really good filmmaker, but he's serendipitous: "Carroll, aren't we shooting this?" "No, I don't want to do that scene—let's do this one." A lot of my crew in Toronto on **The Black Stallion**, who were used to working in TV at the time, thought Carroll Ballard was an idiot, because he did not act in charge and dictate what to do. They thought they were making this stupid, stupid kids movie that's going to appeal to five-year-olds—it was going to be a big piece of crap about a horse and a boy. It was really difficult for me to convince them that Carroll was really talented, and I really wanted to quit. But then I was talking to our sound guy, Nat Boxer, an old pro. He said, "You young guys are all the same—you all think you're making art. I'll tell ya what making movies is about—it's about surviving. You start the movie and you finish it— if ya don't do that, you're full of shit. So don't give me that crap about you're not getting the things you want, or it's not the way you imagined it. I →

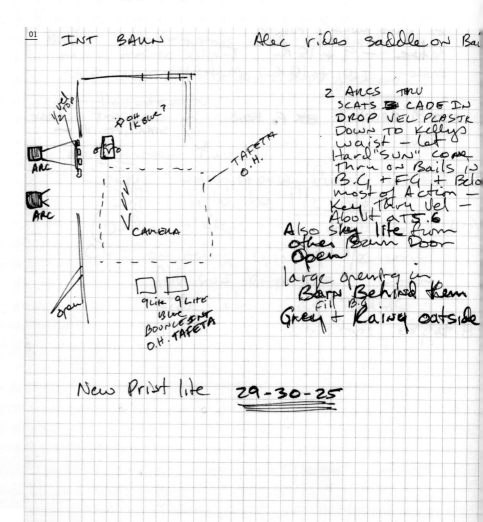

The Black Stallion - Shooting Week #1 July 4-9
printing light 30·29·23.

1st Day Exteriors

Over exposed - BACK LITE SITUATIONS
in field with 600 + 25-250 —
Exposed at T12 , I11 on 600 (64 ASA)
were very hot — /

DAppled light with hot BG. —
Best exposed Close to beat of
BG — T 6.3 (16 ASA)

Clarence in Room — Next to window
-3.5   PUSH 1 STOP
ill 24 f.c. → Start at T4.5   fill with
                grey card to 40 fc or so
hot with   Blue lite
85 on Camera   expose for key lite only —
                When shot the Sillouelled
White Wall   shots had on 3x6 light
Behind Clarence   with Blue Bulbs, Tough
—3½ stops   Rolux + Booster Blue —
Spot read   C.U. had on 6 lights
-5.6 fill to   wide "   "   4 lights away
50 fc   from window

                Exterior was exposed at T9
                reading grass with spot meter
                in field

THE BLACK STALLION

(01–03) "The overriding idea of the movie was that it was from the boy's point of view," Deschanel says about **The Black Stallion**. "For the most part, it's either from the boy's point of view or what you could imagine the boy could imagine. And that's why it has such an intensity to it—you're there with him all the time, and you have an understanding of his emotions, his fears, and his triumphs. Those things are very intimately tied into the aspect that it's really through his eyes."

"I mean, there are times when you just have a horrible time making a movie and it turns out great. Other times when you have a great time, it's a piece of shit."

don't give a crap except ya start it and ya finish it. That's what movies are." And, you know, it's really true. I mean, there are times when you just have a horrible time making a movie and it turns out great. Other times when you have a great time, it's a piece of shit. And there are times when you have a great time and you make a great movie. I mean, you just don't know. But it's nothing if you don't get through it.

Movies are a visual medium. That doesn't mean you can't have **My Dinner with Andre**, which is terrific, but there's not much you can do in a visual context with a movie like that. So that's a factor when I pick a project. If I see a way of bringing something to the lighting and visual style that will help tell the story, then I'm interested. But sometimes, I like the challenge of saying, "OK, this is not overtly visual, but how can I create a visual style that will add something to it?" I just did a film based on a play by Tracy Letts called **Killer Joe**. A lot of it takes place in a trailer. Director Billy Friedkin and I talked about how, when you're in one space for a lot of time, you can create a sense of drama by the changing of time. There's one section of the film that starts late in the afternoon with the sun coming in the windows. We let the sun set, and the sequence gets more and more dramatic as it goes. And then there's this moment of confrontation that happens, and it's basically dusk outside. So it goes from the orangey sunlight to lights on inside with lighted candles. You're able to add some drama by conceptualizing how the light would work throughout the course of the scene. And there are all sorts of things like that that can become elements in the storytelling.

The closest that I can think of to what I do visually is what a symphony does. It's really like music—it has different movements. You create a visual style that really is telling a story—you can repeat certain elements, and then you can bring something new in that's unexpected. A perfect example for me of that is from my mentor, Gordon Willis. In **The Godfather**, every scene is shot at eye level. And then there's that moment when Marlon Brando is in this market and he's about to be shot—and you cut to a high angle that you've never seen in the movie before. You immediately get this sense of dread—something is going to happen. And it's because you've established a visual style that's so solid that when something happens that's different, you go, "Oh, this is different—this is a turning point." If everything is shot from so many different angles, there's no way to create a style that can then be used as a way of telling the story. What's really important to me is to find those elements and to do it in a way that's within the context of the movie and is subtle and works as an emotional point of view and helps advance the story. It's like a character in the movie—it's important for it to be there.

If you think about us as human beings, we're constantly looking at people and trying to judge them. I was reading some interview with a director where he was talking about language—he was saying we invented language so people could lie to each other. The reality is, most of your life when you're having conversations with people, you're judging what emotions they're going through. "They're saying that, but are they really happy? Are they hiding something?" I think we as animals have this incredible instinct to read faces. So many people think they can be actors, but the reason why there are very few truly great actors is because it is really hard to do. Most people don't know what they're giving away when they're talking. Actors are able to act that— some of it is technique, but the best actors I think are, more importantly, instinctive.

There was an actor in **The Black Stallion**, who played the priest on the ship—a really good Italian actor for this small part. But he came up to me and he said, "I act with my eyes." And it's interesting when an actor knows that about himself and you can put a light that brings out their eyes. And so I tend to really watch the actors and I try to figure that out: "Is it their mouth? Is it the shape of their face? Is it their full body language? Is it their eyes?" And a lot of time with actors, it is their eyes.

You must have an understanding of what plane your film works on. **The Natural** is a real archetypal story. All the scenes in the novel →

Knowing when to keep it simple

When Deschanel approached the shooting of **Being There (01–03)**, he heeded the philosophy of his mentor Gordon Willis: Keep it simple. "The whole movie was shot with two lenses—we shot with a 40mm and a 75mm," says Deschanel. "A couple of shots had a zoom, and we had one shot with the 29mm because I couldn't get as wide as I wanted to with the 40mm. But, it's all very simple. And the overriding principle of that movie was that Hal Ashby and I were making a serious film about power and politics. If you wanted to get any humor from that, then you had to get it from the disconnect between the character that Peter Sellers played and everybody else. We expected the audience to do the work—we were not going to present them with a Jerry Lewis comedy with bright lights over the camera and just everything lit. We were going to shoot it with real chiaroscuro lighting and mood, as if it's a serious movie. I think it's successful because it has that visual style—the film really holds up in part because of that."

were taken from real-life stories: the Black Sox scandal, Babe Ruth. **The Natural** literally is a distillation of all the great baseball stories up to that time. So, from the get-go, it's a mythical story—it's about understanding baseball as being a rite that's passed down from father to son. It works on a totally mythical level, and even though there are all these real things that happen—Roy Hobbs gets shot, he comes back, he falls in love, she betrays him—everything's just a little bit heightened reality. And to me, the greatest accomplishment of **The Natural** is that it's taken reality and worked it to the point that at the end of the movie you so desperately want Robert Redford to hit a home run. When he does hit a home run and the lights explode, it's totally believable—but when you think back, it's not real at all. The story had taken the audience and brought them into this mythical world. My part of the story has a lot to do with lighting—everything is just a little bit sharper. It's like somebody being schizophrenic and hypersensitive to everything—it's almost as if you could manipulate nature to the point where everything's in its perfect place.

Over the years, you learn to be as precise as you can about things with your crew, but there's always a slight disconnect because somebody always slightly misinterprets what you say. And lots of times somebody misinterprets it in a way that's better than what you've suggested. That's why I like the idea of films being collaborative, because, if you think about it, an editor might put it together in a way that you didn't think about, but it's better than your idea. Or the costume designer might misunderstand you and come up with something that's much better. That's the great thing about all the creative contributions that go into making movies. And I think there's a danger now because you can have a director being the cinematographer if you want—but then you're missing out on something. I mean, there are some who do both who are good, but you're missing out on the chance of that kind of serendipity and collaboration.

There's so many times you work with directors who ask, "Why do you want to do this shot this way?" You come up with an explanation, but lots of times the explanation is bullshit because the reality is you really just emotionally feel that it's right. I mean, I would literally get sick to my

THE PASSION OF THE CHRIST

(01–02) To find inspiration for director Mel Gibson's account of Jesus' last days, **The Passion of the Christ**, Deschanel looked at many Italian painters. "Both Mel and I really liked Caravaggio," Deschanel says, "and since we were filming in Rome, where there are probably 20 Caravaggio paintings in different places, we could go and study them." Thanks to his wife, who was brought up Catholic, he visited a number of churches, which helped provoke ideas as well. "What struck me was that every church essentially had the storyboard for the Passion depicted on the outer walls. It was amazing: 'There's Jesus on trial, there he is falling, now he's on the cross…' It was so amazing, yet so simple." But Deschanel's own religious upbringing played a part in shaping the project as well. "When you talk about the story that's told in **The Passion of the Christ**, the character of Jesus is mythical," he says. "If you read all the Gospels, there are different points of view about Jesus and who he was. But I was drawn to the story because, having been brought up as a Quaker, I didn't have any real teachings about Jesus and the Bible. For me, it was this great dramatic story of the hero sacrificing himself for the betterment of others. And when you think about it, so much of literature is based on that story. If you look at **Rocky** and many other movies, it's about a character coming back to life."

"I like the idea of films being collaborative, because, if you think about it, an editor might put it together in a way that you didn't think about, but it's better than your idea."

stomach doing something that I didn't feel was right. It's very easy to after-the-fact intellectualize about the reasons you make choices, but in reality I think the creative process is mostly based on instincts. You can explain them later, but oftentimes you are just trying to analyze how you got there. If you study painting, which I did, you'd focus on triangular composition and a sense of perspective and depth—where your eye goes in the frame. But in reality, I think the artist just arrived at that by intuition or instinct—what was pleasing to him or her.

01

02

Raoul Coutard

When the French New Wave's seminal figures are discussed, the most frequently mentioned names are directors: Jean-Luc Godard, François Truffaut, Jacques Rivette, Claude Chabrol. But we should not forget the man who was one of the principal cinematographers of the era, giving the movement its expressive, open aesthetic. He is Raoul Coutard.

Born in Paris in 1924, Coutard had been interested in studying chemistry, but his life ended up taking another path as he became a stills photographer and combat reporter working for, among other publications, *Life*. He spent several years on assignment in Vietnam during the French Indochina War, which would later help shape his shooting of director Pierre Schoendoerffer's 1965 Vietnam war film, **La 317ème section**. Upon Coutard's return to Paris, influential French New Wave producer Georges de Beauregard introduced him to a young director named Jean-Luc Godard. The director was about to make **Á Bout de souffle** (1960), wanting to shoot the movie, Coutard later recalled, "as if we were reporting a story." Coutard's background in photojournalism made him a perfect match for Godard's vision.

The two men went on to make 17 films together, including some of the most quintessential movies of the New Wave: **Le Mépris** (1963), **Band of Outsiders** (1964),

Alphaville (1965), **Pierrot le Fou** (1965), and **Week End** (1967). Moving from the liberating handheld camerawork of **Á Bout de souffle** to the dazzling CinemaScope visuals of the Technicolor tragedy **Le Mépris**, Coutard took to Godard's freewheeling, improvisational style, utilizing location shooting to give the filmmaker's pictures a bracing sense of endless creative possibility.

Coutard's work with Godard would be enough to put him in the pantheon, but he also collaborated with Truffaut, whose **Shoot the Piano Player** (1960) and **Jules and Jim** (1962) represented the more traditional New Wave filmmaker at his most playful and experimental. In addition, he lensed Jacques Demy's **Lola** (1961), a sumptuous love story that made spectacular use of its gorgeous star, Anouk Aimee. But Coutard wasn't simply a phenomenal photographer of the French New Wave. He also teamed up with Greek political director Costa-Gavras for his scintillating **Z** (1969), a canny hybrid of documentary realism and thriller conventions.

Coutard would go on to direct three of his own films, the most notable of these being 1970's **Hoa Binh**, about children caught in the crossfire of the Vietnam War. The drama won the prize for Best First Work at the Cannes Film Festival and was nominated for the Best Foreign Language Film

01 Alphaville

02 Le Mépris

03 Z

Oscar. But Coutard continued to be a cinematographer as well, working with a new generation of innovative French filmmakers such as Philippe Garrel on 2001's **Wild Innocence**.

Now retired, Coutard can look back fondly at a career that emphasized the use of natural light to create vivid, iconic images. And while he doesn't like to simplify the impact of the French New Wave—insisting that each director had his own unique gifts—when asked in a recent interview about which of his own films he considered the greatest, his answer was very much in keeping with the New Wave's pioneering, rule-breaking spirit. "I think that a film is good when you come out of the cinema totally stunned. You have no idea what hit you; you don't remember if you have had dinner or where you parked your car; you want to be alone to think about it. That is the definition of a great film for me."

Raoul Coutard shot several such films and no doubt inspired countless others.

"I think that a film is good when you come out of the cinema totally stunned. You have no idea what hit you; you don't remember if you have had dinner or where you parked your car; you want to be alone to think about it. That is the definition of a great film for me."

04 Bande à part

05 Pierrot le Fou

Vittorio Storaro

"A cinematographer has to design and write a story, starting at the beginning, through the evolution to the end. That's why I consider my profession is as a writer of light."

Vittorio Storaro was born in 1940 in Rome where his father was a projectionist at Lux Film, and at the age of 11, on his father's urging, he began studying at the Istituto Tecnico Fotografico "Duca D'Aosta." He gained a diploma as a master of photography and from the age of 16 to 18 studied at the Italian Cinematographic Training Centre before being accepted into the two-year cinematography course at the state film school Centro Sperimentale di Cinemotagrafia in 1958. At the age of 20 he became an assistant to cinematographer Aldo Scavarda. Marco Scarpelli made him the youngest Italian camera operator at age 21, but a lull in production in Italy slowed his career down before he returned to work as assistant cameraman in 1963 on Bernardo Bertolucci's directorial debut **Before the Revolution** (1964).

He used the long gap in his young professional life to study all the arts. He took his first cinematography credit in 1969 on **Giovinezza, giovinezza** directed by Franco Rossi. In 1969, Storaro was hired as cinematographer on Bertolucci's **The Spider's Stratagem** (1970), which began a long collaboration between the two that continued with the seminal **The Conformist** (1970) and six further films: **Last Tango in Paris** (1972), **1900** (1976), **La Luna** (1979), **The Last Emperor** (1987), **The Sheltering Sky** (1990), and **Little Buddha** (1993). He developed other close director relationships and shot the mammoth **Apocalypse Now** for Francis Ford Coppola in 1978, as well as **One from the Heart** in 1982, **Tucker: The Man and His Dream** in 1988, and a segment of **New York Stories** in 1989. He also worked three times with Warren Beatty—on **Reds** (1981), **Dick Tracy** (1990), and **Bulworth** (1998). Most recently, he has shot six films with Spanish director Carlos Saura beginning with **Flamenco** in 1995, **Taxi** (1996), **Tango** (1998), **Goya in Bordeaux** (1999), **I, Don Giovanni** (2009), and **Flamenco, Flamenco** (2010). He won Oscars for **Apocalypse Now**, **Reds**, and **The Last Emperor**.

Vittorio Storaro

" Cinema is a language of image which is completed at all times by words and music.

It is held up on those three legs. When people tell me I am a painter of light, I say that I am not, because a painter expresses himself in just one single image, likewise a photographer. A cinematographer has to design and write a story, starting at the beginning, through the evolution to the end. That's why I consider my profession is as a writer of light. A cinematographer needs to know literature, music, and painting. I don't mean that you have to become a writer or a composer, an architect or a philosopher, but you have to have some kind of knowledge in order to be more aware of what you are doing. Because when I take a decision with the director or by myself to put the camera in one position or frame a shot in a particular way, we mean something, we are telling the audience something.

If you put two characters next to each other, one in completely full light, the other in shadows, I am telling you if those people are in harmony or in conflict. If you are using a very warm color to dress an actor, that color has an energy which the audiences recognizes not just in their eyes, but in their entire body. They feel an emotion. So without any doubt, if you are using the vocabulary of light or shadows, you are able to write the story with light on film.

To be honest, this wasn't clear to me from the beginning of my career. From the first film I did in black and white, I was mainly aware about light, shadows, and penumbra because that was my vocabulary at the time.

Later, when I did **The Conformist**, I had the idea to build the visual concept into the story. The first part of the story is set in fascist times and is about a character who feels he is different because he shot and killed a man who groped him when he was 12 years old. He felt he was an assassin but hid the true feelings that he was a homosexual and started to act like everyone else, to be a conformist. So my idea was to separate the light and shadows around him, to give him an impression that he was not in harmony with himself. →

THE CONFORMIST

(01) "When we arrived at the apartment where Stefania Sandrelli was living, I had in my mind to do this separation between what was the real life of the character and what he was hiding in himself. I wanted to have the light filtered through the blind, but Bernardo said it was daytime and we should have the blind up. I said we have these strips of light that are creating this kind of visual cage around him, this separation of his elements and he loved it right away."

Color symbolism

Storaro focused on blues to symbolize the protagonist's feeling of freedom when he arrived in Paris in **The Conformist** (01). Every detail was considered, down to the yellow roses, which also convey the meaning of freedom. For **Last Tango in Paris** (02) orange was the color of choice, used to represent the setting sun, and hence the "setting years" of the character played by Marlon Brando.

As the film goes on, the light and shadows almost merge. When he goes to France, I opened the shadows into full light because at that time France represented a place of freedom for Italians. Leonardo da Vinci said that the union of light and shadows created colors, and so I felt that this section of **The Conformist** in Paris should be filled with the color blue, which is the color of freedom.

Two years later, when I was in France doing **Last Tango in Paris**, I was fascinated by the warm color in the early morning which was the combination of the warm artificial lights of the houses and the natural cold light in winter time. I made the connection between the character played by Marlon Brando and this period of his life, and the color orange which represented the setting sun. At the time, I was using this kind of language but I didn't really know the meaning of it. I felt that it was the right thing to do.

When I got to **Apocalypse Now**, I was able to use color to make a conflict between the natural colors of the jungle which represented Vietnamese culture and the artificial color which represented American culture. I was using very strong light at night in relation to the peace of →

01–04 Apocalypse Now

the natural light of the jungle at dusk to create a visual conflict.

When we got to the final scenes with Marlon Brando, I became more conscious of what I was doing. The character of Kurtz was a symbolic element. He was not just a normal human being in the picture, he represented some kind of truth coming out about the horror of the war from the unconscious of US civilization. That was why I placed him totally surrounded by the blackness.

After **Apocalypse Now** I understood that I had to stop working and go away for a year to study, so I could be more conscious about the use of not only light and shadows but what was inside the light itself, and I discovered the world of colors.

I studied painting and literature and architecture in order to become more conscious of the meaning of an image and took a lot of still photographs.

After a full year in my house, I felt I was ready to start to convey that research I was doing into color in film images. **Agatha** was the first film after that and if you can choose a color in **Agatha** it was black because it represents the unconscious of this woman in crisis.

In fact, if I can put it in a figurative way, the journey of the first part of my life is going from darkness to penumbra, to light, and the second part, starting with **Agatha**, went from black to white using all the color spectrum.

The real beginning of visible color was **La Luna**. I remember being concerned when I read the script why Bernardo had titled it **La Luna** when the story is about a mother. When my wife told me that the moon is the symbol of the mother, I realized that Bernardo was expressing himself in a very symbolic way. So I started to read the

Freudian concept of how children connect something they see between their mother and father with colors. From that moment on, a color represents conflict or harmony and each of us see color in a very subliminal way. So from **La Luna**, I started using the symbology of color.

Bernardo and I were lucky in that we almost grew up together. While he was discovering his own way to express himself, that was exactly what I was doing. By the time we got to **The Conformist**, we worked very naturally together. I knew that I had to be completely free to do whatever he was feeling with the camera, and at the same time I was interpreting his movement and his composition with light and shadows as it related to the main concept of the picture. One of the main examples in **The Conformist** is the scene where the leading character arrives in

Paris and goes to visit his old teacher. The teacher is explaining Plato's myth of the cave and Bernardo was explaining to me that he needed to go back to when he was a student to understand the myth. I realized that the only thing for me to do was to recreate the feeling of this cave by turning only one light on and all others off. We came to realize that Plato's myth is a metaphor for cinema: The prisoner is like the audience; the sun and fire outside the cave are like the magic lantern; the people passing by and creating shadows are like the actors on the film, and the back wall of the cave was the screen. I remember there was great emotion doing that scene because, without speaking too much to each other, we were together recreating Leonardo's principle of the camera obscura.

When I first read the two books that Pu Yi →

01–04 The Last Emperor

"My idea was to make the relationship between life and light; different emotions compared to different colors."

wrote on which **The Last Emperor** was based, I wondered how I could represent the journey of this human being. Here was the story of a kid kept in a kind of limbo, who didn't even know that he wasn't the emperor any more. So, because light represents knowledge and consciousness, and light is composed of seven colors, I thought it would be great to see different colors in different moments of his life. So it's like if you have the journey yourself—your memories have one specific color in relation to a certain age, following Newton's color spectrum theory. I brought all this to Bernardo at the beginning of the conception of the film.

My idea was to make the relationship between life and light; different emotions compared to different colors, because in order for him to visualize the journey within himself, I was doing a color journey within the color spectrum. So I gave him a red color when he remembers when he was born as an emperor. Red is the symbol of birth and life. That's why we did it at night so I could use torches and have a very warm color palette. The second color was orange to represent the warmth of the embrace of his mother and the family when he is living in his own house. The third color, yellow, represents consciousness, when he became Emperor. Green means knowledge and this was connected

Inspiration

"I always have the image of Caravaggio's *The Calling of St Matthew* (**01**) next to me because it is a painting that really shocked me when I saw it at the San Luigi dei Francese church in Rome. I had just finished my first film and it was the first painting I'd seen where I could clearly determine the journey of light into obscurity. I wondered how it was possible through all my years of studying photography and cinematography why they had never taught us about painting. This was a painting that changed the entire history of visual art, so is especially important for cinematographers."

The language of color

In **Dick Tracy** (**02–04**) Storaro used the colors in maximum saturation to make them stand out. "We were using mainly primary colors—red, green, and blue," he explains, "and a complementary color like blue/green, magenta, yellow. Color is also its own language in the way that it can be aggressive or not. Even when you put two opposite colors next to each other, like red next to orange, it doesn't mean that one pops out. But red next to cyan jumps out. So we used the dramaturgy of color in **Dick Tracy**."

01

02

to the English tutor coming to the Forbidden City educating him to know what is around him in the world. He arrives in a green car, he gives him a green bicycle and so on.

When he is liberated, we see blue for the first time, which is the color of freedom. When he decides to accept the proposal from the Japanese government to build another empire, he is no longer a child and you see indigo. This is the color of maturity—the moment when you have the chance to use all your physical pleasure and power. The last color was violet, which is when he is in the screening room and he realizes the kind of life he leads and how many people have

died because of his weakness. This is the color of introspection.

When he has finished his education, we put the snow on the floor to represent the color white; the unity, the end of the journey. So we used the entire symbology of the different colors to represent an entire journey.

Only when Bernardo had accepted it did I give the scheme to James Acheson, the costume designer, and Ferdinando Scarfiotti, the production designer. James was surprised because he was planning to use all possible colors in the opening scenes. I told him that we didn't have to not use all the colors, just make →

DICK TRACY

Storaro met with Warren Beatty to discuss **Dick Tracy** on his way to San Francisco to prepare **Tucker: The Man and His Dream** with Francis Ford Coppola. He was not familiar with Chester Gould's comic books but while shooting **Tucker**, happened across a collector of the comics who supplied him with copies of the original series. When back in Rome after **Tucker**, Storaro saw a visual link between the comics and the paintings of German expressionist Otto Dix. "I went to my library and pulled out a German expressionist book and I realized that Chester Gould was influenced by the German expressionists which is quite logical given that one art form in the 1930s influenced another. In particular, the post-expressionists like Dix, George Grosz and Conrad Felix Müller influenced Gould. When I went to LA to meet with Warren and costume designer (Milena Canonero) and (production designer) Dean Tavoularis (who was subsequently replaced by Richard Sylbert because he was busy with Francis Coppola), I showed them the paintings and said that in my opinion the movie should use the main concepts of their work. Everything has to be in conflict between one side of the color spectrum and the other, so some characters belong to the warm, conscious side, and others to the dark side. Dick's costume was the color yellow, which is the color of the sun, of revelation, while his opposite was Big Boy Caprice. Even in the production design and color of the costumes, we were supposed to be using that scheme."

some more prominent. Ferdinando was also a little hesitant at the beginning, but in the end it was wonderful when we did the sequence in the palace in Manchuria with all this tonality of magenta and violet and indigo. So everything fitted very well.

All of the first part of my life is associated with Bernardo Bertolucci, the second with Francis Ford Coppola and the third with Warren Beatty. In 1995, I met Carlos Saura. He proposed that we do **Flamenco, Flamenco** together and I started to introduce myself to Spanish culture and flamenco culture. Carlos was originally a photographer and had mainly worked in black and white. He did movies in color but he was not really aware of the power of colors. He has told me that I introduced him to a new world in colors.

Like Bertolucci, he loved to set the camera

himself, look through the viewfinder, and use the space in one particular way. I started to introduce the color symbology into his images and he was shocked at the beginning. Eventually, I realized that I shouldn't explain it to him verbally, but show it to him. So we were rehearsing a dance in **Flamenco, Flamenco** and he was telling me the kind of camera moves he wanted and I was preparing the lights, not even telling him what I was doing. We started from blackness and with the lightboard that I love to use so I can visualize the entire light structure of a scene. I was showing him the kind of ideas that I had, directly during the rehearsal. He started to really love it. From that point, he started to enter into my vision.

In **Flamenco**, I was mainly using the symbolism of the sun and the moon. When we did **Last Tango in Paris**, he was trying to represent the

REDS

(01–03) Storaro's lighting scheme for **Reds** was to represent the emotions through a soft tonality while the political drama was presented in a naturalistic way. The film was peppered throughout with starkly shot, real-life testimony from contemporaries of John Reed and Louise Bryant. "The visual image to me was like a tree," says Storaro. "The witnesses were like the roots of this plan who were giving us the memory of John Reed. The trunk was like the will of John Reed to be a writer, and the branches and the leaves were like the opening of his mind and the sentiments. The sentiments could be more connected to emotion and were therefore con-nected to colors. So when you see color in **Reds**, it's mainly connected to the love story between Reed and Bryant."

story of his own life in the tango. So every single number had a different color to represent a journey, step by step going down into his own subconscious to reach the beginning when he was a child. When we did **Goya in Bordeaux**, we said now we need to use images on the screen. With the agreement of the production designer, we printed images of interiors onto screens surrounding the actors. They were using just the furniture where they were sitting. The rest didn't exist, it was just an image printed on plastic sheet. We used one color or another to light them from the front or back. This could give you the feeling of the period of the time those characters were living in. Or a completely visionary feeling. Goya was a visionary man, he was an incredible painter. Not only that, but the story that Carlos wrote was once again in connection between his older life backwards. Sometimes we were seeing the same images when he was young and he was old. We changed the way to do art direction and scrapped the scenography altogether.

Working with Carlos has changed his vision, but also my vision.

Working with Warren Beatty

The difficulties of working with an actor/director: When Storaro was hired by Warren Beatty to shoot Beatty's solo directorial debut, the epic **Reds (03)**, the two initially clashed. Storaro had never worked with an actor–director before. "I was used to seeing the scene from an outside point of view and was used to the diction of cinema. To me the camera setup or movement was to do with the language of the images."

Learning to see the scene from the actor's point of view: "For him, because he was an actor first, he thought the camera should move when the actor moves. We fought at the beginning of the picture because I was trying to make him understand that the camera was like a pen for a writer. After I understood that he was used to seeing the scene from an inside point of view, the character's point of view, I started to do the same and began to understand him. We collaborated well after that."

Chris Menges

"You have to be driven, but you also have to listen,
and getting that balance right is what makes you
good or not so good, or good on the film and not
so good on the film."

Born in 1940, Chris Menges is the son of composer and conductor Hubert Menges. He began his career in the 1960s as a camera operator for TV documentaries for directors such as Adrian Cowell and John Irvin, moving on to features such as Ken Loach's **Poor Cow** (1968) and Lindsay Anderson's **If...** (1968). His first film as a cinematographer was Loach's **Kes** in 1969 and he shot Stephen Frears' first feature **Gumshoe** in 1971.

He continued to work with Loach on **Black Jack** (1979), **The Gamekeeper** (1980), **Looks and Smiles** (1981), **Fatherland** (1986) and the more recent **Route Irish** (2010). He also continued with Frears on **Bloody Kids** (1979), **Walter** (1982), **Walter and June** (1986), and **Dirty Pretty Things** (2002). He is perhaps most famous for his two films with Roland Joffé—**The Killing Fields** (1984), and **The Mission** (1986)—which each won him an Oscar.

His distinguished career has also seen collaborations with Neil Jordan on **Angel** (1982), **Michael Collins** (1996), and **The Good Thief** (2002); Bill Forsyth on **Local Hero** (1983) and **Comfort and Joy** (1984); Jim Sheridan on **The Boxer** (1997); Sean Penn on **The Pledge** (2001); Tommy Lee Jones on **The Three Burials of Melquiades Estrada** (2005); and Stephen Daldry on **The Reader** (2008), and **Extremely Loud and Incredibly Close** (2012).

Menges is also an accomplished filmmaker in his own right, and his first film, **A World Apart**, won an acting prize in competition at Cannes in 1988. He also directed **CrissCross** with Goldie Hawn in 1992, **Second Best** with William Hurt in 1994, and **The Lost Son** with Daniel Auteuil in 1999.

Chris Menges

" I've never found it easy to talk about what I do. I like to work in the cinema that I can learn from, subjects that draw me. Those films are not necessarily popular and they're not going to win awards. I don't think the best cinematography Oscar is necessarily the best cinematography of the year, it's to do with being popular.

The best film I ever shot was **Kes** and I wouldn't say that was technically well done at all—I was still learning and a novice then. But the power of that film is breathtaking, I think, so in a way it's not even about the cinematography, it's about what's at the heart of the story, it's about the characters of the story, what a director and the writer are trying to say.

Loach and I had worked on **Poor Cow** together and he felt slightly addled like an egg on the experience of making that film with the producers. After that he said that he was never going to work like that again—we were going to sit back, stay back, and observe the story. We

were going to observe the tension of the piece. The next step, in a sense, was quite revolutionary for us. We liked and respected the work of Milos Forman and Miroslav Ondrícek who had made those great films in Czechoslovakia and we learnt a lot from those films.

On **Kes**, I think Barry Hines' script was very powerful and we learned to stand back and stay outside the circle of the performance. We learned about shooting with long lenses and using natural light, and we learned about how to try and be sympathetic and treat people with a certain amount of dignity.

It's not that Ken was not sure of what he wanted to do—by then he had also made that wonderful film **Cathy Come Home** with Tony Imi, but he realized that on **Poor Cow** he could be manipulated by the "system of cinema." That, of course, is still with us. Cinema is a money-making enterprise and it is compromised because of the money. Of course, you've got to try and get your

IF...

(01) Menges was the camera operator for celebrated Czech cinematographer Miroslav Ondrícek on Lindsay Anderson's 1968 classic **If...** "I have good memories of that film," he says. "I remember wandering around Cheltenham College where we shot and I remember Miroslav saying to Lindsay that he couldn't afford the number of lights needed to light the chapel. Lindsay said 'Well, OK, what happens if we do it in black and white?' And Miroslav said 'We can do that.' And I said 'Won't that look weird?' And Lindsay turned around to me and said 'We'll just tell them it's art and they will think it's brilliant.'"

"On **Kes**, I think Barry Hines' script was very powerful and we learned to stand back and stay outside the circle of the performance."

money back, otherwise you won't get another go, but to be dominated by commercial concerns is surely not the way to make great cinema. Of course, there are always exceptions to the rule and there's no true way. That's why we keep reinventing the wheel.

Having said that, there are such exciting works. I can't think of a single film Vittorio Storaro has shot that hasn't been a magical experience to observe. I was lucky enough to understudy for him on a couple of films. I did some operating on **Reds** and **Agatha** and I watched him work. I recently went to Shepperton Studios to watch Bob Richardson and Martin Scorsese at work on **Hugo** and there are always new tricks to learn. It's a constant thing.

I'm really fascinated by new technology and I think, setting aside 3D for a moment, the Alexa camera is going to be an exciting development. Just the possibility of shooting at 800, 1000 or 1500, or even 2000 ASA gives you more scope.

The argument we are having at the moment is that we only have a digital viewfinder. The thing about operating a camera with ground glass is that you see and understand and believe, and if you don't look through a lens, your conception of what's trying to be achieved is diminished. That's the problem with what they call video village, where a cable is connected to the camera and run to any number of monitors. The director doesn't necessarily have to be on set. For me, the only place the director should rightly be is in the focus puller's way, right beside the camera so he can actually see what the eyes are telling you. You can't understand that watching a video through video village.

The director has to see the performance and say straight after the take that it was perfect or it needs some work. He should be able to turn to the operator and say "Did you get it?" You need those relationships. That's why the cameramen like to operate these days, because they can see with →

02

01 A World Apart

the ground glass. They can see the image and the performance. That's a slight problem with the digital medium at the moment because we don't have an optical finder, we only have an electronic finder.

I'm not a very verbal person and perhaps it's images I can talk with. You can learn from observation and I guess that's what drives me. It's a substitute for verbal communication, I suppose. When I read something, I always go for the story and what I can learn in the process. I wouldn't work on a project that I didn't think was a learning curve, but of course one makes huge mistakes because you never really know what the end game plan is. A lot of it is luck, of course. Like Cartier-Bresson said, you have to walk the streets and if you don't walk the streets, you will never discover anything. We have to walk the streets and we have to propel ourselves into our inquisitiveness.

For instance, I only worked with Alan Clarke once, and that was on **Made in Britain**, but that was a defining moment. He had a really interesting way of working with actors and he challenged me, but he didn't have an ego. He genuinely wanted to capture and explore ideas.

It's only a shortish film and it's the only one I did with him. Unfortunately, when he asked me to do another one I was given the opportunity to direct **A World Apart** and he sadly passed away.

The takes would be several minutes long and sometimes it wouldn't work, but he would just tell you to get on with it. When he came to cut it, it was like editing a whole series of mid-shots. It defies a certain logic in a way because if you are doing a long Steadicam shot there are going to be precise moments that tell the story, but that are not necessarily structured in the shooting for those precise moments if you are chasing around with a Steadicam.

There are no rules, of course, in making a film, and it would be silly to say that something is not going to work. You have to explore it and see if it can work. In a way, photographing a movie is exciting because the opportunities are endless.

I have shot on a handheld camera on documentaries mostly. I made some long trips to Burma with Adrian Cowell in 1964 to make **The Opium Trail**, and again in 1972 to make **The Opium Warlords**. I didn't go with an assistant, so it was just me and the director, who also did the sound. I loaded the mags and did my own focus and I didn't have →

Working as a director

On the four films which Menges directed, he recruited different cinematographers—Peter Biziou on **A World Apart**, Ivan Strasburg on **CrissCross**, Ashley Rowe on **Second Best**, and Barry Ackroyd on **The Lost Son**. "I chose a different cameraman each time," he said. "I think I was secretly trying to learn new tricks, but I did choose people who I thought were really excellent. It's a difficult relationship because no one understands the pressure the director has to go through unless they've done it themselves." Did the experience change his subsequent relationships with directors? "Probably," he says. "It probably did."

01 Filming **Comfort and Joy** (1984)

02 Menges on the set of **A World Apart** (1988)

time to put up a tripod, so lots of it was handheld. I had to be on a long lens because I had to be sure it was sharp and then, of course, you have the dilemma that you can't see the whole story, so you have to manipulate the camera to see everything. So in those films, there is that *verite* thing that Raoul Coutard helped us to understand. In shooting documentaries, you can be much more involved and there's a definite need to shoot the film that way.

The Opium Trail and **The Opium Warlords** were incredibly dangerous and unpleasant because we were stuck in the jungle for a year and a half. Within the Shan State army there were internal coups going on and the Burmese were extremely ruthless to the ethnic people in the Shan, Kayin, and Kachin states.

I suppose Roland Joffé wanted me on **The Killing Fields** because I had spent all that time in Asia being shot at and having my life fucked up. For me, **The Killing Fields** was important because it had something to say about what we →

01–02 The Killing Fields

THE MISSION

(01–03) Although Menges says he feels "a little bit ambiguous about the story" of **The Mission**, he won his second Oscar for the film which was shot in Argentina, Brazil, Colombia, and Paraguay and features the iconic shot of a crucifix tumbling over the Iguazu Falls in Argentina. "We had climbing experts and stunt experts, of course, but the secret to Iguazu is that the Argentinians had built these walkways for tourists that take you all the way around, so while it looks like we were dropped in by helicopter, it was not as difficult from a technical viewpoint as one could imagine. I am not saying the film was not arduous or that the actors didn't take risks, because they did, but it wasn't like being in Burma making documentaries." Menges usually operates the camera himself, but didn't do so on **The Mission** because he was preoccupied with other technical challenges of shooting in the jungle. Instead, his **The Killing Fields** operator, Mike Roberts, took over the camera. "He is a brilliant operator and didn't miss a thing."

didn't know much. We'd read about Cambodia but we hadn't consciously or mentally articulated the experience of knowing it. It was important to me and to everybody who worked on that film in different degrees that the story was told.

Somehow **The Killing Fields** seemed to be more like a personal journey, because of my history shooting in Burma, Tibet and Laos, and because of the work I'd done. Of course it was nothing like the real life of **The Opium Trail** but it was manipulated rather brilliantly.

I think we all tried to create something that felt real and I certainly called on my experience and the use of light and composition.

If you've got a really enlightened director, and a good first [assistant director], a good cast and good people around you, it's not as hard as it might seem to recreate a real period. Roland was really good at knowing what he was after and, although I'd never been in Cambodia, it did have a real feeling of being in that part of the world.

You have to be driven by the story and by the characters, and what they may be thinking—it's really from there that everything comes. It's hard to imagine anything without feeling the characters and what drives them.

When I read a story, I see the way it's got to be told and then tend to get a little bit dogmatic about it. You have to be really careful not to step on anyone's toes, because if you have a vision for something, that's what drives you, and what drives you makes you good at your job, whatever

THE READER

(01–04) Menges took over from Roger Deakins on Stephen Daldry's **The Reader** when Deakins had to leave the long-delayed shoot for a prior commitment. Deakins ended up shooting 31 days and Menges 61 days of the 92-day shoot. "My grandfather came from Germany and I wanted to know about these things so it was a really interesting experience," he says. "The film took a long time to reach production, but when it came to it, the schedule was incredibly tight. I think the opening scenes between David Kross and Kate Winslet were shot in eight days. Stephen storyboarded the court scenes in the second section of the film because time was quite limited and court scenes are not easy because you have multiple points of interest. It's a question of finding a shorthand to tell the story."

01

you do. Therefore when there's a passion, you will lay yourself open to treading on toes, definitely. But without that passion, it would just be a job and you'd take up your exposure meter and wave it around and take the check. You'd be a true pro, but you'd hate yourself for it.

You have to be driven, but you also have to listen, and getting that balance right is what makes you good or not so good, or good on the film and not so good on the film. If you just arrive at work and do the job and go home, you would hate yourself because you would not be driven and not feel that gut-wrenching certainty of how this should be.

I remember when I was about 16, I was a filing clerk and I completely seized up at how boring it was. That happened on films when I was an assistant, I just thought "I can't do this."

I think largely, with two or three exceptions, I tried to go somewhere I'll learn. I don't think I could do my job if I was not in a learning process. I might just seize up. "

Dion Beebe

"We are all there to help the actor do their job. I could have spent two days lighting a set, but if the performance is off, it is just pretty pictures."

Born in Australia but raised in South Africa, Dion Beebe returned to Australia to study cinematography at the Australian Film Television and Radio School from 1987 to 1989. He started his career in features shooting Alison Maclean's **Crush** in 1992, moving onto other notable local films including Clara Law's **Floating Life** (1996), John Curran's **Praise** (1998) and Niki Caro's **Memory & Desire** (1998). His first major production was Jane Campion's **Holy Smoke** (1999) starring Kate Winslet and Harvey Keitel. This led him to bigger international productions including Gillian Armstrong's **Charlotte Gray** (2001), and action movie **Equilibrium** (2002) starring Christian Bale. His career soared when, in 2002, he landed the cinematographer job on Rob Marshall's feature debut **Chicago** which went on to win the Best Picture Oscar and a nomination for Beebe. He has subsequently worked with Marshall on **Memoirs of a Geisha** (2005), for which he won an Oscar, and **Nine** (2009). He has worked twice with Michael Mann, on **Collateral** (2004) and **Miami Vice** (2006), and reteamed with Campion on **In the Cut** (2003). Other credits include **Rendition** (2007), **Land of the Lost** (2009), and **Green Lantern** (2011).

Dion Beebe

"Like most professions, cinematography is about relationships. Yes, you have to acquire a certain technical knowledge (or at least bluff your way through the technical aspects of the job), but people have to be able to invest a lot of confidence in your ability when they are about to undertake a project. You may have a first-time producer or a first-time director, but most of the time, people don't want a first-time DP.

Starting out is hard. I had just left film school and producers wanted to know what other movies I had shot. It's a catch-22. With all the risk involved in making a movie, no one wants the DP to be part of that. They want a sure thing. So for a cinematographer, it's hard to get work when you don't yet have that first feature under your belt. It's about convincing people that you are ready and capable. People do like to lean on the more experienced DPs, so at the start you have to persevere and get the break. You need confidence.

Of course, you also need to prepare thoroughly for every job, particularly on the bigger films with the complicated set-ups—the preparation is always going to help you. It's also about the relationships you develop with your crew and knowing that you can fall back on each other as well as feeling that there's never going to be a situation that you're thrown into that you cannot create a solution for.

When I started out in Australia, all the movies had small budgets, averaging A$1.5 million, and on small movies it is a different mindset. You have a key crew of maybe ten and you have to get everything done with that crew. Often your choice of gear comes down to how much ten people can carry. Within those confines, you are not going to attempt to light three city blocks, you are going to find other ways to do it, and part of the process for me is having a dialogue with the director to find these solutions. As we would →

NINE

(01–04) For **Nine**, Marshall conceived the musical numbers as a figment of the imagination of the lead character, film director Guido Contini, played by Daniel Day-Lewis, and they were played out on a gigantic sound stage built at Shepperton Studios in London. Marshall, Beebe, and production designer John Myhre planned meticulously how the skeleton of the set could transition from number to number and serve different purposes for each. "We built a mock-up of the floor plan for Rob as he choreographed the numbers and placed people, and we would then discuss specific lighting cues and work out the grid position for the lights. No single lighting placement can cover an entire production, but when you are shooting for a couple of months, you have to minimize the number of units. So on **Nine** I worked with lighting designer Mike Baldassari and we worked out three separate hangs: we had one cluster of lights that would cover three or four numbers. We'd re-rig and re-hand for the second set, and again for the third."

01

Lighting the stars

The opening number of **Nine**—Overture Delle Donne—
(**04**) saw Beebe working with a dazzling array of movie
stars in one scene including Daniel Day-Lewis, Nicole
Kidman, Sophia Loren, Penélope Cruz, Judi Dench, Kate
Hudson and Marion Cotillard. Beebe laughs: "It's a sort
of cinematographer's nightmare. If you are working with
a famous actress, you have a certain responsibility. The
cinematographer has to look after them, not from the
studio or actress' point of view, but from the audience's
point of view. If you are shooting Nicole Kidman and
she's a star in a movie playing a movie star, she has to
look fabulous. But we had a lot of people on stage in
front of the camera at the same time and you want to
give them all the attention they deserve. You have to be
able to light them and shoot them all in the course of
two days. We were dreading it. It's not that you expect
anyone to be difficult but, when your attention is across
that many people, it's a lot of moving parts. It was the first
day of the shoot and we had rehearsed and pre-lit, but it
was still a challenge."

> "It makes you understand how important it is to have that dialogue with the director, to work through what's being proposed."

say on set all the time "Improvise, don't compromise." It makes you understand how important it is to have that dialogue with the director, to work through what's being proposed.

I remember on **Memory & Desire** with Niki Caro we were shooting in Japan and it was impossible to get permission to shoot on the subway. We had an important sequence in which the main character, whose husband has recently died, is crammed in a train in rush hour. It was a moment of being surrounded by people but feeling completely alone. Our solution was to cut holes in shoulder bags, insert our camera with the lens out of one hole and the viewfinder out of the other and smuggle the gear into the subway. We carried handheld lights and went in knowing we had about a ten minute window before someone stopped us. We shot the entire sequence like that, but looking at the film now, you wouldn't know it. These moments come out of necessity. The other solution would have been to shut down the train, clear the platform, and

bring our own people in, but once you do that, you are committed to a big expense for a scene that is about mood and atmosphere. It will be an uphill battle to convince a producer to spend limited resources on a scene with one character and no dialogue, yet these are often the most memorable and poetic moments of any film.

Some directors like to focus on the technical aspects more than others, but a knowledge of aspect ratios and lenses is really not as important as the ability to tell a story.

A movie like **The Insider** (1999), a story about a whistleblower in corporate America, doesn't sound terribly tense or thrilling, but what Michael managed to do—and I think that's his signature—is to create unease when you watch it. We've all done the handheld shot behind a character walking down the hallway, but what Michael did in **The Insider** was place the camera literally on the hairs of Russell Crowe's neck. He broke through into the personal space of the actor and suddenly the audience felt as vulnerable in →

CHICAGO

(01–03) Beebe worked with director/choreographer Rob Marshall on **Chicago** and had to design lighting and shooting plans for 17 musical numbers. "I would work with Rob as he was choreographing the numbers so we developed them as they were being choreographed. We talked about the lighting, the color, and the positions, and were looking at the grid system, and how many units of lighting we needed, and how many we could afford."

We used two to three cameras on each number, but on some of the bigger ones, like Razzle Dazzle, we went to four. While there was some value in the fourth camera, we found that three was the best number for us because Rob is very precise about what he wants to see, and when he wants to see it, particularly with the dance. If he's got a big lift or a big turn, he wants to see it from a specific angle or head to toe."

All the numbers were challenging because of lighting and it was very helpful to have great theatrical lighting designers working with me. The lighting became part of the choreography, as on Cell Block Tango where we introduce each of the characters very precisely with a stab of light."

Marshall and Beebe worked closely together on effective transitions between the drama and the musical numbers, which were a figment of Roxie's imagination. "We wanted interesting ways to get in and out of the numbers," says Beebe. "We used very theatrical devices. We used lighting nets from the front and faded through them, for example. And then we'd do things like bring lighting cues into a real environment. So when Roxie goes into Funny Honey, the cop is shining a flashlight in the face and that turns into a spotlight beaming into her face to do the song."

> **"What is exciting about working with first-time directors is that they will often have these requests that have no consideration about cost or practicalities."**

terms of periphery of vision as that person does. As Crowe walks through his house at night, you are enormously tense and you're not quite sure why, and yes, there is music, but mostly he creates tension just using the camera.

In **Collateral**, I particularly remember one situation where we were shooting Javier Bardem having his conversation with Jamie Foxx in this odd backlit nightclub. Javier is sitting at a table and behind his head is an arrangement of succulent plants. They are long, pointed, and with jagged edges. In many cases they would simply be set dressing, but for Michael they became a counterpoint to the conversation and to Javier's character. The angle, placement, and lighting of that single element took a good 45 minutes. I had my key grip, Scott Robinson, up on a ladder manipulating cutters to achieve the exact amount of menace from those plants.

Michael is definitely a perfectionist and he will often focus intensely on something like that because it is important to him: it's part of the composition and the storytelling and the tension of the moment. It might seem misguided because, hang on, shouldn't we be getting on with this scene, but you realize when you see

his work that that's part of how he makes his movies. That ability to create tension through the composition of the frame and the juxtaposition of elements within it to support that is signature Michael Mann. I have memories of Michael on the back of a low-loader car traveling at 40mph and he is pushing down on the shoulders of operator Gary Jay as he watches the on-board monitor, all in pursuit of the perfect frame.

Rob Marshall is a filmmaker with a strong vision and it's my job as the cinematographer to facilitate that. "No" is not an option with Rob, and nor should it ever be. If there is a shot, as in **Memoirs of a Geisha**, where he wants the camera to be flying over the rooftops and end up at a window on a little girl looking out, you find a way to do that.

What is exciting about working with first-time directors is that they will often have these requests that have no consideration about cost or practicalities. I think this is important. The idea is the key, and having these blue-sky moments liberates those ideas. Yes, we always have to consider how and for how much, but not before we consider what that idea hopes to realize on screen. We should never discourage a grand vision. →

MEMOIRS OF A GEISHA

(01–04) After **Chicago**, Beebe and Marshall reteamed on the epic drama **Memoirs of a Geisha**, which would win Beebe the Oscar. A set of the Japanese town circa 1920 was built in southern California, principally because, Beebe says, no such town still exists in Japan. But Beebe's biggest challenge was getting the light correct, both inside and out. "We started testing it from the very beginning and you're in a period where there would be a mix of some electric light and oil lamps. We knew we wanted a sort of burnt, amber light inside because of the oil lamps and the tarnished patina of the walls—they'd been burning these types of lamps inside these walls for years."

Shooting Japan in California

Don't overwhelm the fabric colors: Beebe established the color and gel combinations of the lighting and then worked closely with costume designer Colleen Atwood to ensure that the fabrics weren't being overwhelmed by the light. "Colleen would often go back and re-dye and strengthen the colors, in order to offset the warmth of the light and not lose the colors in the costumes."

Control the sunlight: (03–04) For lighting the exterior, Beebe was aware from the start that the film would require all four seasons of light—including snow in winter, leaves changing in autumn, and cherry blossoms in spring—and the California sunshine would be wildly incongruous. "We came up with the idea of silking the entire town, which was a silk cover about the size of two football fields," he says. "The silk would basically control the sunlight, and allow us to create winter. There is a sequence in the film where the camera moves over the snow-covered rooftops and this was shot on a sunny Californian day. Literally beyond our silk was hard sunlight."

Prevent the panels from tearing: Beebe explains that the silk softens and controls the light and meant that he and his team could eliminate the hard, direct light. The panels of thick white silk overlapped each other like sails on a ship to avoid capturing any gust of wind, and operators sat in the rigging during the day to monitor wind speeds and control the panels and prevent them from tearing. The total cost of the silking of the town was $1m.

COLLATERAL

(01–02) Beebe worked twice with exacting director Michael Mann—first on **Collateral** and then on **Miami Vice**. The film was shot on the VIPER camera. "Working in the digital format for the first time was an amazing experience because you could line up a camera on the streets of LA at night and see buildings silhouetted against the night sky. You couldn't do that on film at that time. The big challenge is that you are almost working backward with a camera that sensitive. You set up your camera to capture as much of the background as possible and then you start bringing in your actors and it has to feel completely seamless and unlit, yet it has to be lit. Traditional lighting didn't work. Any sort of backlight or hard key just felt fake and, of all the tools in a cinematographer's chest, knowing when something feels wrong is your biggest asset. So we worked with ultra, ultra soft lighting fixtures in order to light faces. For the first time, my meter was useless. We were working at levels where my light meter couldn't register a single dot. It became about studying it, trying to match colors to the streetlights, finding a way of making it seamless, and making it feel like the environment was lighting the actors. When your environment is almost entirely self-lit, you've got to work harder and more subtly to illuminate your actors."

In the taxi cab sequences, paper-thin photo-luminescent panels were rigged throughout the car. "Getting into that cab and working with this rather odd light source was a quick education," he says. Perhaps the film's most celebrated scene is when a coyote strides quietly across a street in full glare of Jamie Foxx's taxi cab. "Doing that scene was sheer madness," recalls Beebe. "We shot earlier dialogue sequences with Tom and Jamie and then rushed off down Olympic Boulevard to get into place because it was 3 or 4 in the morning and we were holding up traffic. We had animal wranglers there, and cameras in the middle of the road, but when you release a coyote onto the streets you don't really know what it's going to do.

"The camera was in the hand but they are never locked off because Michael likes to capture a moment of unease. He feels handheld is imperceptible unless you are chasing someone, but you do feel the energy of the operator in the frame lines. So we had two cameras in the hand, and it was a crazy moment, but for me it is the defining moment of that film, and that's what Michael brings to a script. He can visually define the movie in one image. That scene says everything. And that's the thing, it's those moments in a film where everything seems to connect and line up."

MIAMI VICE

(01–02) Whereas **Collateral** was a combination of film and digital, with most of the night exteriors shot on digital, **Miami Vice** was subsequently shot entirely on digital in locations around Miami and Latin America. "He chases authentic locations and, in my experience, he doesn't shoot on stages," says Beebe. "And when you take these big films on location, there are many challenges. On **Miami Vice**, for example, we were in the Dominican Republic doubling for Paraguay. We went into the slums, recruiting the local gangs as our security, and we had to lock down this big open square and control it at night. I had to find ways to work in this place, run power, and rig lights. We started prepping it months ahead in order to nail down the logistics of locking it down, powering it and creating that authentic environment that would exist if none of the crew had been there. It was not a safe environment."

> "I feel that my job with actors is to make them feel as comfortable as possible in that very odd environment of a film set and to create an atmosphere of trust."

Rob was like that on **Chicago**. He had a very clear vision of that film and was not inhibited at all, or intimidated by the technology or the equipment. We had a tight budget, but never let that dictate the type of film we wanted to make. In the end, a clear vision, some great actors, and lots of detailed prep helped achieve a great deal.

I feel that my job with actors is to make them feel as comfortable as possible in that very odd environment of a film set and to create an atmosphere of trust. We are all there to help the actor do their job. If, for whatever reason, an actor is off their game, then the film suffers. I could have spent two days lighting a set but if the performance is off, then it is just pretty pictures.

I will therefore afford actors whatever they feel they need, whatever strange quirks or foibles they have. However upset they might get on a set or seemingly upset, you have to realize how hard it is for them. I'm not the one stepping up in front of the camera delivering lines and having to believe in this false environment.

I often find myself in the midst of a film standing on the actors' mark and looking back at the camera. Instead of my usual view of the set which is framed through the lens, carefully composed and lit, I am looking from the other side. This view of the set is a mess, with lights, stands, and flags, cameras pointing at you and people standing around on cell phones and eating bagels. The dressed set, composed frame, and carefully crafted lighting that is presented through the camera, is not what the actor sees. Instead they look out at this mess and have to center themselves and not just believe this environment is real but make us believe it too. Often all an actor has is the other actor, often off-camera, to help them make that connection. Some actors will not stay for off-camera work. However, most I have worked with will. My favorite actor's off-camera moment was on the movie **Nine**. I had been so focused on this tight push-in on Daniel Day-Lewis that when I finally looked over toward camera to comment on

IN THE CUT

(01–03) To create a mood of paranoia, fear and awakening sexuality in Jane Campion's **In the Cut**, Beebe came up with some camera tricks. "We used swing shift lenses—a sort of bellows—which allows you to manipulate the lens independently of the camera body. That allows you to create and control planes of focus, so by swinging the lens off on an angle, you create a plane of focus that runs diagonally across the frame as opposed to flat to the frame. So suddenly you have an element deep in the background and close to the foreground in focus, but the top right of your frame and the bottom left are completely soft. So we were able to focus on what Frannie (played by Meg Ryan in the film) is focused on. It's a way of eliminating the periphery and showing very specific details within the frame. About 70 percent of the film was shot with these lenses, which, combined with handheld, meant we could move through these environments and focus on what we wanted to see and nothing else."

something, I realized that Daniel had arranged the greatest off-camera acting ensemble ever gathered. There were Sophia Loren, Judi Dench, Penélope Cruz, Marion Cotillard, Fergie, Kate Hudson, and Nicole Kidman crammed up next to the camera. My camera operator was beside himself, but it goes to show the importance the actors place in having that connection with one another on the set.

Probably my biggest influence was Sven Nykvist. I first saw **Cries and Whispers** when I was in my teens and without even understanding the film, I became aware of Nykvist's work. Together with Bergman, who was such a powerful storyteller, they created some of the most lasting sequences ever captured on film. Another big influence of mine was Robby Müller. **Paris, Texas** was a defining film of its time and Müller's use of natural and mixed light sources was inspiring. He made use of the new high-speed film emulsions of the time and shot with single florescent fixtures and small practical lights. The use of color to

create depth, and the huge natural landscapes in that film still influence my work today. 🙴

Jack Cardiff

Jack Cardiff is widely acknowledged as the cinematographer whose experimentation with the new format of Technicolor created some of the most influential color images in the history of cinema.

Born in 1914, he was a child actor and appeared in his first silent film (**My Son, My Son**) at the age of just four; he found his vocation behind the camera at the age of 15 when he started working as a clapper boy and camera assistant at British International Pictures.

By 1936, Cardiff had become a camera operator at Alexander Korda's Denham Studios. It was then that he was chosen to be Technicolor's first trainee in the UK on the basis of an interview in which he professed technical ignorance, but a fascination with how painters used light to achieve certain effects. He operated camera on the first film to be shot in the UK in Technicolor—**Wings of the Morning** (1937)—and was mentored by US cinematographer Ray Rennahan. He also traveled the world with 16mm travelog filmmaker Count von Keller shooting films in three-strip Technicolor in Europe, Asia, and Africa.

During the war, he shot several documentaries with the Ministry Of Information's Crown Film Unit including the Oscar-winning **Western Approaches** in which he had to cram the unwieldy three-strip Technicolor camera onto lifeboats and ships to shoot the action.

It was a fortuitous job as second-unit cameraman on Michael Powell and Emeric Pressburger's **The Life and Death of Colonel Blimp** in 1943 which would start a partnership that would define Cardiff's career. Powell was so impressed by his work on **Blimp** that he hired him as cinematographer on **A Matter of Life and Death** (1946), the epic post-war fantasy which he shot in both color and black and white.

Black Narcissus followed in 1947. Set in the Himalayas but shot entirely at Pinewood Studios outside London, the film confirmed Cardiff's painterly eye and his debt to Vermeer, Turner and Caravaggio. His use of light, shadow, color and movement in creating the expressive visual mood for the pent-up drama and repressed sexuality of the film was striking and won him an Oscar.

The third and final film he shot for Powell and

01 Jack Cardiff
set of **The Afri**

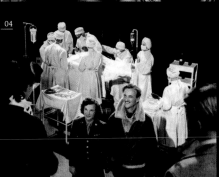

Pressburger—**The Red Shoes** in 1948—took his experimentation with color and light to even bolder levels. The classic film, set in the world of ballet, included the stunning Robert Helpmann-choreographed Red Shoes ballet, and Cardiff came up with numerous ideas to add visual excitement from changing the speeds of the film when shooting the dance to dramatic close-ups on the dancers—no mean feat bearing in mind the size of the Technicolor camera.

Although he wouldn't work again with Powell and Pressburger, Cardiff went on to create other works with great directors—with Alfred Hitchcock on **Under Capricorn** (1951), which featured dizzying long takes around complicated sets, and with John Huston on **The African Queen** (1951), which was shot on a river boat in the Belgian Congo. His career took off from then and he shot a series of dazzling Technicolor movies in the 1950s, both in Hollywood and the UK, including **Pandora and the Flying Dutchman** (1951), **The Magic Box** (1951), **The Barefoot Contessa** (1954), **War and Peace** (1957), **The Prince and the Showgirl** (1956) and **The Vikings** (1958). He became renowned for his ravishing lighting of screen goddesses from Ava Gardner and Marilyn Monroe to Sophia Loren and Audrey Hepburn.

His close relationship with actors and his keen interest in serving the story led him to direct his own films, first on B-movies like **Intent to Kill** (1958) and **Web of Evidence** (1959) and then,

famously, on **Sons and Lovers** in 1960. His film of the DH Lawrence novel, set in a northern English mining town and shot, ironically, in black and white, won seven Oscar nominations, including one for Cardiff as director. His cinematographer Freddie Francis won the Oscar.

He focused on directing throughout the 1960s but when the UK film industry almost ground to a halt in the 1970s he made a decision to return to cinematography and his output was as busy and diverse as ever taking in action movies including **Rambo** and **Conan The Destroyer** and epic TV mini-series **The Far Pavilions** and **The Last Days of Pompeii**.

He died in 2009 at the age of 94, but by then his legacy had been truly recognized. He was the first cinematographer to win the honorary Oscar in 2001, and a feature-length documentary on his career—**Cameraman: The Life and Work of Jack Cardiff**—was released in 2010 to great acclaim. It featured extensive interviews with the likes of Cardiff aficionado Martin Scorsese and Powell's widow and Scorsese's editor Thelma Schoonmaker.

02 The Red Shoes

03 The African Queen

04 A Matter of Life and Death

05 Black Narcissus

Owen Roizman

"I used to like to think that I didn't have a particular style, but then I noticed that when people were hiring me for films, they wanted a certain thing that I did. There are many different words to describe it, but the one I like to use is 'realism'—not documentary realism, but an aesthetic that feels real, like a heightened realism."

A modest man who lensed some of the most iconic movies of the 1970s and '80s, Owen Roizman grew up in New York and began his career in commercials before transitioning to film, although he continued to helm commercials in between his film shoots. The son of a cameraman and the nephew of a film editor, Roizman first came to the industry's attention as the director of photography on two classic William Friedkin films, Best Picture-winner **The French Connection** (1971) and **The Exorcist** (1973). From there, he became an in-demand cinematographer on landmark '70s pictures such as **Play It Again, Sam** (Herbert Ross, 1972), **The Heartbreak Kid** (Elaine May, 1972), **The Taking of Pelham One Two Three** (Joseph Sargent, 1974), **The Stepford Wives** (Bryan Forbes, 1975), **Network** (Sidney Lumet, 1976), and **Straight Time** (Ulu Grosbard, 1978). Starting with 1975's **Three Days of the Condor**, Roizman began a long creative partnership with director Sydney Pollack, which continued with **The Electric Horseman** (1979), **Absence of Malice** (1981), **Tootsie** (1982), and **Havana** (1990). He also has collaborated several times with writer–director Lawrence Kasdan on **I Love You to Death** (1990), **Grand Canyon** (1991), **Wyatt Earp** (1994), and **French Kiss** (1995). A past President and current Vice President of the American Society of Cinematographers, Roizman received the organization's Lifetime Achievement Award in 1997. Throughout his career, Roizman's films focused on a realistic portrayal of their worlds, even in science-fiction and horror movies such as **The Stepford Wives** or **The Exorcist**. Roizman has been nominated for five Academy Awards in the span of 23 years.

Owen Roizman

"Mine is not the kind of story you normally hear—it's not the glamorous, passionate, "I grew up with a camera in my hand, and all I ever wanted to do was take pictures" story. My father was a cinematographer, working as a newsreel cameraman for Fox Movietone News for 22 years—he worked as a camera operator on a couple of TV series, such as *Mandrake the Magician* and *Sgt. Bilko*—but I didn't visit him on set that often. And my uncle was an editor—he was nominated for an Academy Award for the short film **Rembrandt**—but I had no idea what he did. My true love was baseball. I was a baseball player, and I had a couple of tryouts with the Yankees. I was a good player, but I also had polio when I was 13, and it left me with one bad leg, which ended my hopes for a baseball career before it even started. I went to movies as a kid, but baseball was what I really cared about.

I studied math and physics in college—I figured I'd be an engineer or a mathematician. I went for interviews with a lot of companies in my senior year, and I asked, "How much money would I make?" I remember this one guy said, "Well, you'd start at about $5000 a year, and if you do well, in three to five years you could probably work your way up to maybe $7500." So I thought, "Hmm, that doesn't sound like a lot." I then asked my father how much money I could earn as an assistant cameraman, and he said, "Well, if you work a reasonable amount, you can probably make about $10,000 right away." I said, "That's what I'll do."

I'd already had good preparation to become an assistant cameraman. During the summers in college I worked in the camera room for a very large camera rental company in New York. We prepared the cameras for rental—we'd have to check all the lenses, check the mechanisms, and make sure everything ran properly. I got to learn the mechanics of the camera, which is what an assistant cameraman does. Then my father gave me my break—he was working on commercials at the time, and I worked with him on some of

TOOTSIE

(01–02) Tootsie is one of the most beloved comedies of the 1980s, but Owen Roizman remembers that it wasn't an easy shoot. "Dustin Hoffman was just obsessive," Roizman says. "He kept coming in every morning with new pages that he rewrote the night before with Murray Schisgal. Then when Sydney Pollack would start blocking the scenes with him, Dustin would tell Sydney that he had another way to do it." Needless to say, that caused enormous tension between the director and star, but for Roizman his job was clear. "You let them hash it out," he says. "I still had to do what I had to do, and try not to take sides." As for shooting a comedy, Roizman didn't change his approach from the way he photographed dramas. "I never thought, 'I have to shoot it funny.' You might show a little more body in comedy because sometimes it can be better to stay back and see some of the nuances of body language, but I never shot a comedy any different than I would shoot anything else. I always took the approach that the laughs are going to come from the writing—they are not going to come from what I do visually, although

I certainly can help enhance them in some cases." And no matter the on-set friction, Roizman appreciated Hoffman's work ethic. "The best actors, you never have to say to them, 'You're a little off your mark here.' They know what to do—they know to match from one shot to the next so that when you edit the movie, their dialogue and body movements come at the same time in every take of each camera angle. As much of a pain in the ass as he sometimes is to work with, Hoffman is a total pro—he's always aware of the camera and that his responsibility as an actor is to match and to do things technically correct. And you appreciate things like that—many others often don't have a clue, and you want to strangle them."

01

"With anything, the first break is really important
—that's when you've got to be lucky and have
some connections."

them. He spoke to some friends who gave me a chance to work with them. With anything, the first break is really important—that's when you've got to be lucky and have some connections. Of course, after that first break, it's up to the individual to come through if you want to get called back.

Nowadays, people go to film school, they graduate, and they become cinematographers. But in those days, it was an apprentice situation where you start as an assistant, you work your way up to camera operator, and then work your way up to director of photography—it would often take many, many years. I did not love being an assistant cameraman because it meant schlepping around a lot of cases and equipment—it's the hardest job on the set. It's all a mechanical job, but you can learn by watching the people above you to prepare yourself for moving up into those positions. So I wanted to be an assistant for as short a time as I possibly could. I was 27 or 28 by the time I became a director of photography

on commercials, and that's really early—usually around 40 or older was the age where somebody would move up from camera operator to first cameraman or director of photography. So I did it very quickly, and it was because I was ambitious and I just didn't want to schlep any heavy equipment around and do all that mechanical work.

I used to like to think that I didn't have a particular style, but then I noticed that when people were hiring me for films, they wanted a certain thing that I did. There are many different words to describe it, but the one I like to use is "realism"—not documentary realism, but an aesthetic that feels real, like a heightened realism. I always liked when people asked me, "Did you shoot **The French Connection** with all available light? After all, that's the way it looked." And I would say, "Absolutely—whatever was available from the lighting truck, that's what I used." In other words, I lit just about everything other than the day exteriors. But I'd light with the thought in mind of "I'm going to try to make →

02

"Magic was my hobby—I loved magic, I loved to fool people—so I always thought, 'OK, I'm going to light this in a way that will make other cinematographers wonder where the hell I put the light.'"

it look unlit." Now, if I was shooting today with the equipment that we have now, I'd probably set most of it up so that I could shoot without any light. In those days, the lenses and the film were slower, so to make something look like it wasn't lit, you still had to light it—otherwise you wouldn't have an exposure. Magic was my hobby—I loved magic, I loved to fool people—so I always thought, "OK, I'm going to light this in a way that will make other cinematographers wonder where the hell I put the light." It was like a little game I played in my own mind. So I'd say my style, if anything, was making it look real, or natural.

Take **The Exorcist**. One thing Billy Friedkin and I talked about from the beginning was, in order to really make it work, we shot it not to look like a horror film. It had to be something that felt believable. I mean, Billy has never referred to **The Exorcist** as a horror movie to this day. The audience sitting there shouldn't be aware of tricks, and that's how you subconsciously draw the audience into the story—by making them feel that they're witnessing something that could be happening. In the case of **The Exorcist**, we wanted to keep it very believable.

In **Tootsie** I did the same thing—Sydney and I talked about not making it look phony. We wanted the audience to say, "Yeah, I could see that these characters would accept that this ugly man could be a woman." I love working in that style—when I was a kid and I'd go to a movie, I wasn't aware of the lights and cameras. I just felt like I was there watching something. If I had seen behind-the-scenes pictures of the crew and the cameras, that would kill it for me. I always felt like I was there—like, "Did they even use a camera for this?" I was always intrigued by that feeling.

I was very selective about the film projects I chose when I started out. There's a question of financial security when you accept or turn down work: Do you have enough money to feed your family? I always had commercials, so I had a way to earn a living even if I wasn't shooting a feature. And actually, I started directing commercials as far back as the mid-'60s—that allowed me the freedom to pick up a script and say, "Do I want

to spend three months on this? Would I go see it in the theater?" If the answer was no, I wouldn't shoot the movie. I only averaged about one-and-a-half features a year—I could have worked nonstop without a break if I wanted, but I didn't want to. In between features, I shot commercials—to me, commercials were like being on vacation, as well as a great training ground. I wanted a life—cinematographers don't seem to have lives now. When you're on a film now, it's all encompassing—you don't have time for your family. I find that very frustrating, and I don't understand it at all. The long hours that they work nowadays are ridiculous.

Network was the best script I ever read—without question, bar none, no comparison. I called up the producer, Howard Gottfried, and I said, "This is incredible! I have to shoot this movie!" I would have been heartbroken if I didn't get to shoot that film—that's how much I loved it. Sidney Lumet would know what lens he wanted to use on every single shot for the entire movie before we ever came on set the first day—that's how clear his vision was upfront. But in the script, you could just picture all of it. Paddy, the scriptwriter, would write, "Shafts of light are coming in the window and the curtains blow and the guy is standing there and there's a beam of light…" Paddy wrote the visuals, and Sidney didn't change that—he just wanted to get on film what Paddy was writing. It was all written for us, so I would just go do it and make sure it ended up on film. That's why the screenplay was so important to me—I've always felt it's about the writing. If you have a good screenplay, that's your base. It's hard to screw up a good screenplay—and it's almost impossible to make a good movie out of a bad screenplay.

Grand Canyon was another movie I loved working on. Partway through the movie, we were shooting one scene, and it was a very tender and emotional scene. I just leaned over to Kasdan and I said, "Larry, I don't know if ten people will come see this movie when it is released, but I have to tell you, you're making a great movie." Everything about it just felt right. It was in the script. I could →

THE EXORCIST

(01–04) Beyond its power to terrify, **The Exorcist** remains a masterclass of exceptional makeup work, which posed unique challenges for Roizman. "During the early stages," he recalls, "it just wasn't working. Dick Smith, our makeup artist, was patient and kept going back and trying different things, but for some things that looked OK to your eye, you'd say, 'OK, this works,' but then you'd put it on film and it wouldn't react to film the same way. It might be something in the film emulsion, or the colors in the makeup itself, so we shot several makeup tests." Of course, part of the difficulty in crafting the transformation of Linda Blair's character was that there were no real-life examples from which to compare the makeup, so the creative team had to go on instinct. "We relied on believability," says Roizman. "Some of the early makeup tests with the cuts on the face and things like that, just looked like a joke. If you were there in the room with that creature, you'd have said, 'This looks like something that was put together by a makeup artist.'" One of the problems was that even after Smith came up with the look for Blair's makeup, it would require several hours each morning to reapply—and the look might subtly shift from day to day. "It just wouldn't respond quite the same way," Roizman recalls, "and I was working really hard to make sure that everything stayed consistent on my end. It was crucial for me to use the same lighting units, at the same color temperature, and the same intensity and exposure every day. The makeup was all done by hand with great skill, but there's always human error that can occur. Fortunately, it rarely, rarely ever happened, but if it didn't feel right, Dick Smith was such a great guy and you could talk to him. He had no ego about it—he'd see it too, and he would go and make it work, because he's an artist."

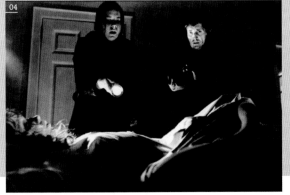

see the sensitivity and the passion that he put into the making of it. And it was a great cast—Kevin Kline is a prince, and Mary McDonnell was just fantastic. It was a terrific group of people, and everybody seemed to be loving it—with a Kasdan movie, when you're on the last day of the movie, everybody cries that it's over. Nobody wants to see it end—that's the way his movies are, whereas some you're like, "Wow, I can't wait for this to be over with and get the hell out of here." **Grand Canyon** wasn't a big hit, but I can't do anything about that—you do the best you can do on the movie, and the rest of it is in the movie gods' hands. Something that may be appealing to me might not be appealing to somebody else. Sometimes a picture is well-written and it still doesn't do well at the box office—that's the enigma.

I'd always prepare with some kind of visual plan, but I didn't like to refer too much to films that were done before—I didn't want to copy them. (Sometimes I would refer to other films to make sure I didn't do it like that.) Probably one of the most extensive preparations I did was for **Wyatt Earp**. I was going to be shooting some day-for-night in that movie, so I rounded up

as much past day-for-night shooting as I could. Plus, I grabbed some old films where I just liked the lighting. In those days, these were on LaserDisc—I could freeze a frame and make a snapshot of that on my video printer. I put these all in an album—both good examples and bad examples. Larry Kasdan and I sat and compared images—what we liked and what we didn't like. We created a visual blueprint of the path we wanted to take, just to have as a reference: "Hey, this is an image I really like—I have to remember this." If you saw that album now you'd say, "But **Wyatt Earp** doesn't look anything like that." That's because I didn't necessarily write down ideas—I did it mostly from feel, from memory. The album was just a collection of images that I liked, to be used as references.

I always joke that I never got hired to shoot a film based on an interview—I rarely went in there bubbling with enthusiasm. If it was a script that I loved, there was no way I was not going to get the job—I would find a way to talk my way into it somehow. But if it was one that I thought, "It's good, it's OK, but I don't know," I usually wouldn't get that movie, because I wasn't that enthusiastic about it—I think maybe it showed through. I'm →

THE FRENCH CONNECTION

(01–07) For the gritty crime thriller **The French Connection**, Roizman operated the second camera, which was usually handheld. "I didn't want to operate any camera on feature films," Roizman says. "I had too much to do looking at the lighting and spending time with the director. It's not like today where you spend time at Video Village and you don't have direct contact with anybody."

Locations with restrictions

Only one light: One of the most famous scenes in **Network** (01) involves Peter Finch's madman broadcaster Howard Beale coming face to face with Ned Beatty's Arthur Jensen, the mysterious chairman of the network's powerful parent company. Across a long conference table, Jensen loudly lectures Finch about the "natural order of things today," which is that corporations, not nations, rule the planet. "We shot that in the New York Public Library," Roizman remembers. "They didn't want us to hang any lights at all, but after a little begging they let us rig one little light, on one post, on the opposite end of the table from Ned Beatty so I could get some light on him."

Be creative: The restrictions forced Roizman to get creative. "I put lights all around the floor to light portions of the walls so that when Ned Beatty walks down the length of the table toward Peter Finch, I could silhouette him in certain places and highlight his face in other places. Normally, you'd hang lights from above, but I had to put them on the floor. I felt like I was in handcuffs, but I was really happy with the result."

When you're your own worst critic: Despite the scene's iconic look, Roizman confesses he would do part of it differently if he had the chance. "I wouldn't have had Beatty as bright at the end of the table during his speech," he says. "It was a little too overexposed for me. I'm my own biggest critic—probably a lot of cinematographers are. I'll look back at some of my films and I'll say, 'What was I thinking when I did that?' A still photograph from that scene hangs in the boardroom at the Academy of Motion Picture Arts and Sciences, and every time I see it, I think, 'Ah, if it was only a little darker…' "

01

not the best when it comes to verbalizing and articulating my passion for a project, so I probably was a turn-off to a lot of people when I interviewed with them. Good or bad, right or wrong, that's the way I am, and I always had the attitude of, "Hey, my work is what speaks for me." I always preach, "It's not what you do or say on the set, it's what's on the screen that counts—that's you." Save the ego stuff for someone else— there's your ego right there on the screen. So I figured people were going to hire me for what they saw, not necessarily for who I was.

Maybe it helped me in my career that being a cinematographer wasn't a childhood dream—I had less anxiety about it. I remember when I got my first nomination, for **The French Connection**, I thought, "Wow, I got a nomination? Man, I fooled them." And then when I got my fifth nomination, a friend of mine called to tell me the news and said, "Well, guess what? You fooled them again." I said, "Yeah, when are they going to catch on to me?" I always took that humble attitude—I never shot a film with the intention of trying to get an Academy nomination or anything like that. To me, that was just the byproduct of working hard, doing a good job, and staying true to the story. I just always thought, "Wow, I'm lucky to have this job, and as long as they don't catch on to me, I'll just keep doing it."

GRAND CANYON

(01–02) Although the emotional, multi-character storyline of **Grand Canyon** lacks showy cinematography, Owen Roizman received one of his biggest compliments on the film from a colleague. When starting out in the 1970s, Roizman became friends with fellow cinematographer Conrad Hall, and would pick his brain: "I loved his work. He was one of my idols." They remained friends, and after **Grand Canyon** came out, he received a call from Hall. "Connie says, 'Haskell Wexler and I just went to see **Grand Canyon**, and all I can tell you is, boy, have you come a long way since that guy that was picking my brain back then.' That was the nicest phone call I ever got." Below (02) Roizman adjusts the blinds prior to shooting the cafe scene.

Barry Ackroyd

"The art of cinematography is to concentrate the audience's minds and create a reality for the audience to inhabit. The aesthetic ensures the viewer is a participant observer. The act of viewing remains active and politically engaged."

British cinematographer Barry Ackroyd is celebrated as a pioneer of the documentary realist style of filmmaking, working with a naturalistic, handheld approach to cinematography. This has characterized the look of films he has worked on, such as **United 93** (2006), **The Hurt Locker** (2008), and a dozen Ken Loach films.

Born in 1954, in Oldham, in the industrial North of England, Ackroyd began his journey at the Rochdale School of Art, where he undertook a multidisciplinary art foundation. Sculpture became a major influence, molding his way of seeing, and providing a kinetic understanding that he applied to animated and experimental films. He then completed a degree in film at Portsmouth Fine Arts College, where realism and the French New Wave heavily influenced the course. In 1976, Ackroyd moved to London, and after struggling to join the Film Union ACCT, found freelance work with the BBC, working on documentaries, and taking jobs to troubled regions where no one else wanted to work.

Ackroyd spent the next decade shooting documentaries, covering a variety of themes and visiting over 50 countries. In 1987, he filmed his first narrative feature; Henry Martin's **Big George is Dead**, for Channel 4 Television. Shortly after, he received a surprise phone call from Ken Loach, which led to the 1991 award-winning film, **Riff-Raff**, and a subsequent 20-year collaboration. This resulted in a dozen films, including **Raining Stones** (1993), **Ladybird Ladybird** (1994), **Land and Freedom** (1995), **Carla's Song** (1996), **My Name is Joe** (1998), **Bread And Roses** (2000), **The Navigators** (2001), **Sweet Sixteen** (2002), **Ae Fond Kiss** (2004), **The Wind That Shakes the Barley** (2006), and **Looking for Eric** (2009).

After seeing **Out of Control** (2002), Ackroyd's collaboration with Dominic Savage, Paul Greengrass asked Ackroyd to work on his film **United 93**, which led to their collaboration on the 2010 film, **Green Zone**. In 2008, he worked on **The Hurt Locker**, with Kathryn Bigelow, for which he won a BAFTA, and Oscar nomination. In 2010, he worked with Ralph Fiennes on his directorial debut, **Coriolanus**, which premiered at the Berlin Film Festival in 2011.

Barry Ackroyd

" When I start shooting, I try to create a mood, visually manifesting the essence of the script, aligning the collaborative process of filmmaking, transforming words into moving images, and capturing a single vision. The reviewers of **The Hurt Locker** praised the film's verisimilitude, and recognized a new level of realism, which helped lead to its overall success.

I have always been conscious of realism's association with political intent, and have worked with this notion in both my documentary and narrative filmmaking. I see no distinction between a political documentary and a political film, in that the aim is always to capture humanity through my cinematography.

I was first drawn to cinema through films such as Ken Loach's **Kes**, and the cinematography of Chris Menges, both in his documentaries and his narrative film work. I have long been enthralled by cinema, but my experience of cinematography has always been practical. I know about the classic "key light, back light, fill," but the rest of it has been a process of experience, trial, error, and observation, an attitude I believe suits the nature of film. I have always been more interested in the personal than the technical. I believe cinematography is about the ability to interpret what you see, not simply to record it, and to infuse an image with vitality and emotion.

When I was shooting documentaries, I filmed everything from the Russian space mission to the demise of the AWB (Afrikaner Resistance Movement), from the obscenely rich to the unfathomably poor. With Nick Broomfield, with whom I did four films, we took a subjective, investigative approach to documentary filmmaking. Instead of indulging in the traditionally disingenuous objective approach to documentary making, we set out with an aim, structured by our initial understanding of the subject. However, the final documentary was constructed by chance encounters and unforeseen events. We allowed the people, the place and contingent experiences to mold and construct the story, producing a story shaped by the subject, rather than individual bias.

The first requirement to work as a freelance documentary cinematographer was to own a 16mm film camera, a 10:1 zoom lens, and a set of four prime lenses: 9.5mm, 12mm, 16mm, and 25mm. I didn't have enough money for the full kit, so I bought a second-hand Aaton camera, and

UNITED 93

(01–02) For **United 93**, Paul Greengrass' extraordinary retelling of the hijacking of United Airlines' Flight 93 on Sept 11, 2011, the fuselage of a plane was taken to Pinewood Studios where it was placed on a gimbal, a pivoted support that allowed the rotation and rocking of the plane.

"We had a very strong brief for the visual aspects of it," explains Ackroyd. "We had a rock-and-roll-style rig where we could move a whole rig of lights on a computer so they could be raised up and down, left and right, so we got an impression of the plane moving. We also had a timeline that coincided with the path of the sun. We knew, for example, that it traveled north on the runway, then taxied and came round onto the south runway, and took off into the southeast, so we knew where the sun would be at what time."

In addition to the lighting and the visceral handheld feel he is known for, Ackroyd says that he suggested to Greengrass to shoot in long takes using multiple cameras. "Because it happens in real time, I thought we should make them do the whole thing all the way through. We could shoot for four minutes because we had four-minute magazines on each small, handheld camera but we would start with Camera A for two minutes and then B Camera would come in, and then we would have two shots going for the next two minutes. We had hidden some magazines down the seats along the way, so when Camera A ran out, we could reload while Camera B was still shooting. There was no missed stuff. You would just drop down and get in between the seat, get your breath back and reload."

three stills-camera lenses: 35mm, 50mm, and 85mm. This contributed to me creating a different look. Without the standard required kit of wide-angle lenses, I had lenses that were more varied. I handheld the long lenses, creating a more dynamic kinetic that provided more choice for the editor and director. It was this more dangerous approach that helped me form my distinct style, and led to my understanding that the best visual effects are focus, exposure, and choice of lens.

I now usually choose to work with zoom lenses, the Optimo 24–290mm zoom, which I used on **Green Zone**. Zoom lenses allow you to use depth of field and mess with the focus; you can move from wide-angle shots to direct close-ups, directing the audience and leading them in, building tension by reframing and refocusing. I always believed the best shots in documentaries were the ones that were out of focus, or under-lit—the imperfect, but necessary image, highlighting the inherent element of chance, a quality that I love. It alerts the viewer to the act of the filmmaking process, and replicates the act of seeing. I have always loved Pennebaker's **Don't Look Back**, which I believe

embodies this approach. It's the feeling that that moment is the only moment. Commercials and films now try to recreate this out-of-control aesthetic, but under controlled conditions. For me, the aim is to lose control.

Ken Loach taught me a lot about the filmmaking process. It's about being responsive to your surroundings, giving space to the actors, and shooting with the minimum equipment; simplifying it all. If you can create a natural setting through a series of reductions, it is possible to get closer to reality. On the first three films with Loach, I watched and listened to what he wanted to do, and enhanced it as much as I could. In a scene in **Riff-Raff**, I remember deciding to bring in a 2.5 HMI light for some extra bounce, but Ken remarked on it affecting the actors. I quickly took it away, and discerned that less was definitely more. I learnt that a harmonious balance between the performance and the craft is what makes a good film. My response was to develop techniques to build lights into the set, so that the lighting became part of the fabric of the film. I began putting Kino Flo tubes into cutaway downpipes. It's low-tech, easy to disguise, and adjustable, but →

GREEN ZONE

(01–03) One of the most spectacular sequences in Paul Greengrass' Baghdad-set action thriller **Green Zone** is the climactic night chase in which Matt Damon's US army officer is in pursuit on foot of an Iraqi general, while US special forces pursue them both. Told from multiple perspectives, the sequence runs up and down stairs, through buildings, and down dark streets.

"We ended up shooting that whole sequence four stops underexposed, which the film stock is not meant to be able to do," says Ackroyd. "When we were grading it, we would freeze frame every frame and each looked like a Magnum photograph of war at night. I was confident that we had achieved our aim, but the production company, Working Title, was worried about whether

the audience could take it. They had already gone through Paul's crazy camera storytelling on the **Bourne** films and we were taking it to another level."

Ackroyd and his gaffer Harry Wiggins had a plan of the section of the city that was used for the chase and where the lights would have to go **(03)**. "We literally filmed over a six-acre area outside Rabat in Morocco for all of one night and it was all underlit," he explains. "I thought of doing day for night, I thought of gelling the lens so that it looked like green night vision and shooting on night vision. We went through a lot of things. But in the end, it was just underlit and captured."

"Paul's brief was that it was a city under attack, in curfew with no generators, no lights, no lights on the

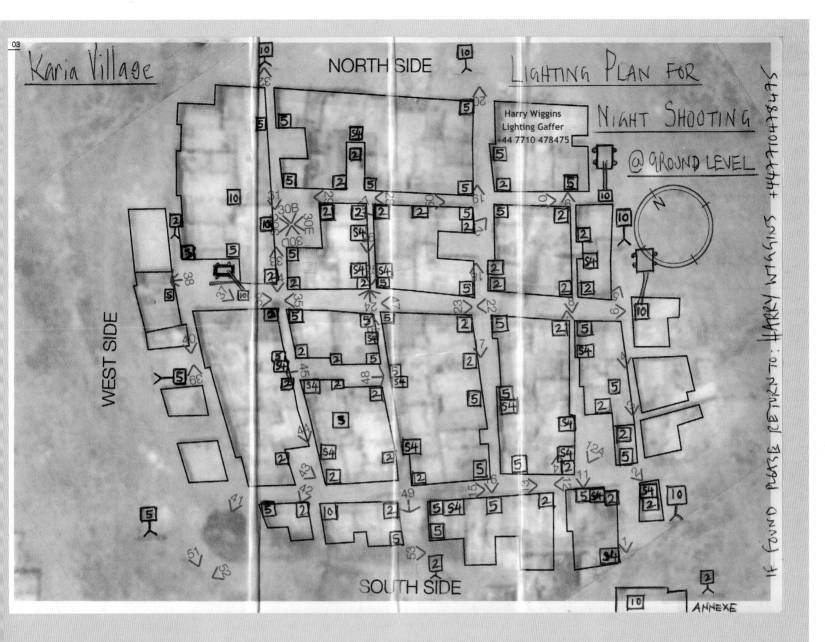

guns, and that's what we had to capture." The sequence was lead actor Matt Damon's last work on the film before leaving the following day for another shoot, and Ackroyd's team had to get it right. "He had to run out of this building, through this, down there, around the corner, dash to that corner, run and get jacked in the car, and drives away. We could have done it in a series of single shots, or we could set up with the special-effects team to do it in one take."

The effects team rigged flashing lights from gun shots and explosions to take place at specific moments in the chase and Ackroyd planned the exact route for Damon to run. He ran with him and shot him as he ran, then another cameraman picked him up as he came through a specific gate and shot him on a Steadicam as he ran down a street. A third cameraman picked him up as he turned another corner. "We used three cameras," he says. "I finished my shots, took another route through the alleys, and came back to pick him up to get the fourth angle. I am very proud of that sequence," he smiles.

> "I always operate my own camera. I think it is fundamentally important; it means that I am there to capture welcomed surprises."

you can hide them behind a desk or a cabinet, or lie them on the floor.

It's the approach that I acquired from working with Ken Loach, that I have been able to hand on to Paul Greengrass and Kathryn Bigelow; providing space for the actors, keeping the lenses discreet, and not breaking scenes down, but allowing for long takes that capture the complete performance.

From working with Greengrass and Bigelow, I have been able to develop a more open, personal approach. I have started using multiple cameras, multiple perspectives, and zoom lenses, to evolve a distinct kinetic. By working with a variety of directors, I have been encouraged to keep my practice energized and inventive.

Greengrass first approached me after seeing Dominic Savage's **Out of Control**, a film about young offenders. Savage researches his films as if they were a documentary. He then populates them with actors and non-actors, to fashion a series of scenes that reflect actual events and scenarios, creating part-film, part-documentary, a

method I really like. This approach parallels the method of Greengrass, who also works from primary sources of recent significant events, such as Bloody Sunday, 9/11, or the Iraq war. The handheld aesthetic is necessary to the documentary feel Greengrass sets out to evoke.

I always operate my own camera. I think it is fundamentally important; it means that I am there to capture welcomed surprises, and can maintain a consistency within the process. I worked out early on that there are only three factors to cinematography: the light, the subject, and the camera. It is by moving the camera that you can make the strongest images and feel the human connection with the subject. As a cinematographer, it is your role to create this dynamic between light, subject, and camera; therefore I believe it is important to be in control of the lighting and the mechanism of the camera. If you have the camera in your hand, you can make little adjustments to constantly changing conditions. Using a handheld camera means you become an unobserved observer, responding to

LAND AND FREEDOM

(01) Ken Loach's films are never shot handheld but always on a tripod at eye level. However, Loach allowed Ackroyd freedom within his rules. In the dramatic collectivization scene in Spanish Civil War film **Land and Freedom**, Ackroyd was challenged with shooting a large debate between 30 people in a room.

"We don't have monitors on the camera, Ken doesn't have a monitor, we don't record it, and we don't have playback," says Ackroyd. "So everything is on trust. I remember we were listening to everyone speaking in different languages and throwing the camera back and forward, and all these different names being shouted. That was off a tripod but we would move. The first time we did it, we kept the camera running so that we didn't lose sync, and would just take one lens off and put another prime lens on, so change from an 85mm lens to a 135mm lens, while leaving the camera running. That's not considered a very good technical thing to do but you do it because you don't want to stop the performance."

Ackroyd explains that by changing the lens mid-sequence, he could get closer in to particular actors. "So we move in a few feet and put on another lens. The focus pullers didn't have any marks to go by. It was all done by judgment in those days. Now they have cinetapes and sonic devices to find out where the camera is pointing. It all helps, but they are only aids."

01

the action, whilst remaining unobtrusive. Greengrass loves traveling shots behind people's heads, so the audience feels like they are intruding on a conversation, inciting action. We would often shoot through doors, encouraging people to start moving around in their seats to look through a door frame, or peer through the keyhole. Inspiring this physicality of the audience comes from the camera's physical participation with the scene, a quality that can only be achieved with the camera in your hand. I love the relationship between seeing and doing, hand and eye coordination. My left hand is really active, moving between the zoom, the aperture, and the focus.

Throughout my career I have always used film. Bigelow was unafraid to use Super 16 and to visit real locations. This attitude suited my style of working, and confirmed my interest in **The Hurt Locker**. Bigelow and I both revel in the artistic quality of film, and its painterly nature. Film has a tangibility, and the magic of light exciting chemicals produces a quality particular to film, marked by its iridescence and intensity. The →

Working with Ken Loach

Ken Loach's filmmaking modus operandi involves only telling actors what will happen to their characters as the story progresses. In **Raining Stones**, the mother and her daughter are baking cakes and preparing for the girl's first communion when the debt collector, to whom the family is in debt, comes to the house and threatens them. But the actresses were unaware that the debt collector was on his way.

Creating spontaneity on set: "We baked cakes all morning long and then Ken said we should take an early lunch," recalls Ackroyd. "He had it all worked out and sent the actresses playing the mother and daughter back to get lunch. We all stayed behind and brought in the other actors. After lunch, we started baking cakes again with the little girl, and I repositioned the camera in the corridor so we could see the door. There was a knock on the door, and the guy bursts in! The mother had no idea it was coming. It's always on film, there are no rehearsals, and once the actors know what's happening, we do it again. We get both shots."

The acting sometimes determines the action: Ackroyd recalls a scene in **Bread and Roses** in which a woman tells her sister that she had worked as a prostitute to support her. "The actress didn't know and you saw the reaction on the face and you are behind the camera and you were in real pain—they were breaking down." In that instance, Loach actually changed the direction of the scene based on the reaction of the actresses. "She was meant to leave her but the actress said that there was no way she would leave her sister at that moment."

01

01 Ackroyd with Ken Loach on the set of **Riff Raff** (1991)

16mm cameras, I feel, enable the free-est approach to making a film, allowing the use of long zooms. These allow good interaction, necessary for an energetic narrative. However, for the slow motion shots, we used the high-speed digital Phantom camera. The use of the hi-speed mixed with live action, gives a film another element.

On **The Hurt Locker** we chose to use four cameras simultaneously, which is usually considered to be a limitation due to lighting. It is usually better to have lights in one direction, than multiple directions, but I will try to light a scene to accommodate any potential angles. However, with an experienced team of camera crews, who all understood the style we were trying to achieve and knew to keep any lights out of shot, we managed to get added coverage, which made each scene seem to exist in 360 degrees.

Film is a beautiful art and a beautiful collaboration between people; that is what I love about it. Filmmaking is about everyone coming together and getting inspiration off everybody. To have an interesting crew is really important; a team, who support and communicate with each other, and motivate, inspire, and energize each other. And importantly, a group of people who you can sit with and talk film, because nearly everybody I have worked with in the film industry, works in the industry for one reason, and that's a passion for film.

I always wanted to work with cameras; I knew this is what I was going to do. I have always felt myself as a filmmaker; part of the collaborative process, and the link between the director and the crew.

I believe film to be the greatest art form. It's a rewarding process of creatively stimulating your imagination, to produce this beautiful physical thing. While no one art form can change the world, you should always try to do that with every film. „

THE HURT LOCKER

(01–04) The four cameras that Ackroyd was in charge of on **The Hurt Locker** shot over a million feet of film between them. "We used lower technology in a sense because we used Super 16 cameras," he says. "Kathryn said she didn't want any high-tech cameras getting in the way. We wanted to give the impression of 360 degrees to the audience. You think you are in the street with these guys as they walk down it to make the bombs safe, and you see every corner of the street, every rooftop, every gutter."

One of the many riveting sequences in **The Hurt Locker** sees the EOD team investigate a car full of explosives that has been left outside the U.N. building. Ackroyd explains: "We had one cameraman on the roof because the actors were all in different positions. Then we had a camera with Brian Geraghty who was going

Shooting an explosion

The opening explosion in **The Hurt Locker** that kills Guy Pearce's character was shot in slow motion and conceived by Ackroyd.

Shoot in slow motion: "I'd done a documentary called **Kaboom** and had photographed in slow motion a huge explosion reconstructed in the desert, so I knew that there was this bubble of energy at the core of it. In those days we shot in 16mm with very high-speed syncrosonic cameras. You put the camera behind a steel wall and set off the real bomb and this bubble of air comes forward. So when I read the script of **The Hurt Locker** and the scene with Guy Pearce talking about the kill zone, I thought we should recreate 'the bubble.' We could do it with CGI, but we didn't have the money. We had just heard that the Phantom camera had come out, but a guy in Lebanon had made a camera like a Phantom, which they were using for a lot of commercials and which is perfect for slow motion. So we got this camera and invented some shots to tell the story. The top of the car was just going to explode and we put some more dust and rust on it. We put the camera at the highest speed we could and it worked great."

backward and forward, and I was inside the car with Jeremy Renner's character. If there is a place where there will only be one camera, I will put myself there first because I know from my background that I can capture that. I like to walk away and know that the scene has been covered."

Ellen Kuras

"Images need to mean something. They need to tell a story. There's a big difference in making imagery— just doing the shot—and telling the story."

Growing up, Ellen Kuras had many passions, ranging from Egyptology and sculpture to sports. In her professional life, she's proven to be just as eclectic, shooting features, commercials, concert films, and documentaries with equal aplomb. She's incredibly determined: her own documentary, **The Betrayal** (a story about what happens to a Laotian soldier and his family when the US abandons its allies after the Secret Air War in Laos), was begun as a Master's thesis film in 1984, yet she continued to follow her subjects for the next 20 years.

Her work on feature films began with **Swoon** (Tom Kalin, 1992), which won the Excellence in Cinematography Award, Dramatic, at Sundance. Her lensing is marked by its intimacy, and she's enjoyed a fruitful collaboration with Spike Lee on **4 Little Girls** (1997), **He Got Game** (1998), **Summer of Sam** (1999), and **Bamboozled** (2000). She has worked with director Michel Gondry on **Eternal Sunshine of the Spotless Mind** (2004), **Block Party** (2005), and **Be Kind Rewind** (2008), balancing the filmmaker's whimsical spirit with a graceful, lived-in quality that gives his films an emotional resonance. Kuras has also collaborated with writer–director Rebecca Miller on **Angela** (1995), (for which she won her second Best Dramatic Cinematography prize at Sundance), **Personal Velocity: Three Portraits** (2002), (for which she won her third Best Dramatic Cinematography award), and **The Ballad of Jack and Rose** (2005). Kuras is the only person to win the Sundance award three times.

In addition, she has been a part of some of the most memorable music documentaries of recent times, as the director of photography or working as a cameraperson on **No Direction Home: Bob Dylan** (2005), **Neil Young: Heart of Gold** (2006), **Berlin** (2007), and **Shine a Light** (2008). She continues to work as one of the few women cinematographers in the studio world, having shot **Blow** (2001), and **Analyze That** (2002).

Ellen Kuras

"As a child, I was very interested in ancient and classical history—interested in how the ancient world developed through engineering, through ideas. So when I entered university, I went intending to be an Egyptologist, although I had many different interests in other disciplines as well. I decided to go to Brown University because I could shape my own program in the open curriculum that Brown offered at the time. Given my interests in different areas, I thought it would be much more academically appealing to me to put my own program together: courses in philosophy and English, and courses in history and social anthropology.

Film was in the back of my mind for many years, but I didn't really pursue it as an idea. My mom was actually a movie buff who would watch old black-and-white films on TV late at night. When I was a kid we had one movie theater in town, and oftentimes the same movie would play for a month or two. I ended up seeing **2001: A Space Odyssey** and a film called **Billy Jack** maybe four times each. What struck me in Kubrick's **2001** were the images—the fundamental story of evolution and the light. They were so visceral, so pure. I was in awe. What struck me about **Billy Jack** was that this was the first time I saw a cowboys-and-Indians movie that was told from the side of the Native Americans. I had always had this kind of inherent sympathy for what has happened to the Native Americans. I was interested in how much **Billy Jack** enabled us to have a glimpse inside of the culture and teach us about the situation without being didactic. How a feature film could actually inform you and spur you to look for more information was a realization I had at a relatively young age. Even though I was just a kid, I was already inspired by the power of film to open up your mind.

The Rhode Island School of Design happened to be right down the street from Brown University, and as Brown students we could take two classes

SWOON

(01–04) To prepare for her first feature film, the black-and-white drama **Swoon**, Ellen Kuras shot Polaroids. "I used them as my guide," she says. "I learned how to read the Polaroids for what I would get, and to understand where I was at in terms of the blacks and the highlights. I have to say that now we have many more tools to check our work as we go along, but early on I used to be terrified in dailies. You think you know what you're doing, but sometimes it's like, 'Oh my God, I'm not sure about that.' If one thing is off photo-chemically, the entire thing is off. That's what makes film exciting." **(02)** A page from Kuras' extensive shot lists for the film.

01

"I wanted to be involved with films that would carry a political message, but move me emotionally."

a year for credit. I always had, more or less, an artistic sensibility—I was always making things in my father's basement. I was very interested in sculpture and was inspired by my father who was a very creative person as well. So I wanted to take a sculpture class at RISD, but there was no room in the class, so I ended up taking photography instead. That move changed my life. Looking through the viewfinder and really looking at light for the first time, to see how light reacts, what happens when it goes through glass, or what happens when it goes through a window shade—I completely fell into another world and fell in love with discovering it. I wanted to spend my time in the darkroom and make photographs. Because I had an 8x10 enlarger at the school, I was able to start sandwiching negatives and creating different kinds of collage with still photography. So, naturally, I then became interested in movies. At the time, I was going to a lot of movies; I was very influenced by **The Battle of Algiers**, **Missing**, and **Z**, and the animated

films of Eastern Europe. I thought, "Well, this is a really interesting way to send a message to talk about the nature of the world and the human condition." I wanted to be involved with films that would carry a political message, but move me emotionally.

These ideas led me to look at the idea of propaganda and how propaganda can work to subjectively influence how we see the world, to impart a certain message. In other words, how is meaning created? How do images tell stories without words? I was looking at a lot of photography at that time and wanted to understand how images and color affect our perception. When we look at an image, compositionally and graphically, how does that affect us? What do we see first in the image? Is a subjective point of view really propaganda, because we invite the viewer to see how we're seeing in a certain way? I spent a year in France doing a lot of very intense theoretical study, but I realized, even with all the theory, that I wanted to get my hands on →

02

```
SWOON SHOT LIST

DAY ONE

Scene 4, D/E   VENUS IN FURS
                FLS
1)   Extreme long shot of drop matching the horizon, Germaine and
     Susan standing in place, Richard and Nathan walk out of
     frame

2)   Series of singles, two and three shots orchestrated to allow
     all the walk bys

3)   Possible shot of Valda's line about feeling the lash with
     her on one end of moving dolly, camera on the other

(I'll flesh this scene out ASAP)

Scene 3, D/E  MARSH SCENE
                    LS
1)   Establishing long shot of Nathan, Richard at a distance

2)   Nathan POV, bird watching, Richard at a distance

3)   Richard POV, eating, Nathan at a distance

     all shots from tripod

--------------------------------------------------------------
DAY TWO                    must be done by 9 pm.

Scene 16, D/E  MURDER SCENE

1)   Moving car shot of Nathan, Richard and Bobby in car

2)   Backseat handheld shots of murder including:
          -hand over Bobby's mouth
```

03

04

Ellen Kuras | Interview **137**

"Images need to mean something. The images themselves need to tell a story."

a camera. I didn't want to talk about something; I wanted to make something with meaning.

The idea to make a film about the story of the Secret Air War and the Laotian people emerged from a desire to tell a complex story about US foreign policy and the loss of values in our society. I didn't want to make a typical documentary that talked about people; I wanted to make a film that could show a world view, through which the audience could vicariously experience a moment or moments in the life of another and how they see themselves in the world.

I started making **The Betrayal** before I became a cinematographer, but soon realized that I needed to try to shoot the film myself to discover what I was looking for. For the first five days of the shoot I hired a cinematographer who was recommended to me. I talked to him about some of the ideas that I wanted to capture: making connections within the family relationships and also seeing certain connections to the culture. When we looked at the dailies, the footage was very nicely shot, but I realized that there was something missing. Only through picking up the camera myself did I realize that it was the meaning. Images need to mean something. The images themselves need to tell a story. There's a big difference in making

imagery—between just doing the shot—and telling a story with how the camera moves, where it moves to, when to rack focus, and how to use light. There's a reason behind making these decisions. In a sense, I was looking for how to make images that could be visual metaphors for the story. This was a realization that has influenced me to this day and made me a much better cinematographer. Even now, I mentally think about the story I'm telling even if making a simple move with the camera.

There's a different kind of prep that goes into feature films than goes into a documentary. But the approach to each genre sometimes crosses over as in, for example, location scouting. Even if I'm shooting a documentary, I try to location scout as much as I can. With a documentary, I want to know what the story is, I want to learn the background, to read materials about it, and to know the approach. When I go into shooting a documentary, I have to be the eyes and the ears of the director, and I have to be the editor, because I'm editing in camera—I have to make sure that I get the coverage that's necessary for them to cut it together. For me, knowing the story is vitally important because I have to know what story I'm trying to tell with the images—I'm creating a significant part of the story with the

THE BALLAD OF JACK AND ROSE

(01–02) Ellen Kuras has shot three films for writer–director Rebecca Miller, their most recent being the intimate family drama **The Ballad of Jack and Rose**, where much of the action takes place in Jack and Rose's home. Kuras says, "Rebecca and I have become so close in terms of how we communicate that with **The Ballad of Jack and Rose** sometimes she'd be sitting there in the room down the hall and I would be shooting, and at a certain point I was beginning to zoom in just as she was thinking, 'Zoom in now.'"

PERSONAL VELOCITY

(01–02) "I have a very special relationship with Rebecca Miller," Ellen Kuras says. "She and I are quite the symbiotic collaborators in our perspectives and the way we see things." They worked together on **Personal Velocity**, a series of short stories about three separate women facing individual crises. "We prep a lot—Rebecca and I will spend hours talking about a film and sitting down and writing out ideas and writing out the shot list and what we want to do. Much of what went into **Personal Velocity** was about how the visual could help to tell the story—the way it's shot, whether the camera moves or not." From their conversations came the idea of including insert shots within the narrative and still images that Kuras refers to as "macro epiphanies… these glimpses into a person's state of mind or their place in the world." In **Personal Velocity**, these moments helped make internal mindsets visual. For Kuras, these pre-production discussions also helped solidify the film's thematic paradigms. "I work really well when I'm able to talk about things intellectually and thematically. It also dictates my style—not only creating meaning, but also determining what is the theme and what's the subtext. I operate much more along the lines of subtext than I do along the lines of straight text."

camera. So I need to know a lot before I walk into any situation. Also, I want to know what I'm getting into in terms of the lighting and what I can do to influence it—maybe putting the subject by a window, or getting in a certain position where I can shoot it a little bit better. There's a lot more prep that goes into documentaries than people think. Documentary is not objective—it's very subjective. Everything that we shoot is a choice. How you shoot it, when you shoot it—you're just not turning the camera on the subject.

Swoon was the first narrative fiction film that I ever shot. It was in black and white, a period film, and was supposed to be a 40-minute art film. We shot the first ten days and then we realized we had a movie, so we went back and shot four more days. I didn't really know very much about dramatic film at that time. I'd always

looked at dramatic film with awe: "How do they know how to do that?" When I sat down with Tom Kalin, the director, we very much shared a common language. He also came from a theoretical background. We concocted our shot lists yet ended up stealing a number of shots throughout the shoot because we didn't have a lot of time for coverage and because I was always looking for moments when the actors were in character but unaware of the camera. That's where my documentary experience kicked in.

At first, I didn't really trust myself on **Swoon**, because I'd never shot a dramatic scene before. I was just starting out as a director of photography, so I called up a DP friend of mine, and I said, "How do you know that you're doing the right thing and not screwing up?" He said, →

Creating natural light

Working only with natural light: When director Michel Gondry hired Ellen Kuras to be his cinematographer for **Eternal Sunshine of the Spotless Mind (01–03),** he was insistent that he didn't want to use film lighting. "He felt that if he wasn't using film lighting it would make it more simple, and natural," Kuras says, smiling. "And I said, 'It doesn't work that way—sorry, honey.'"

Hiding the light bulbs: Gondry's desire and stylistic preference compelled Kuras to find creative ways to light the film's set practically, hiding light bulbs around different parts of the set. "I allowed the actors to not have any marks at all, which put the camera assistants in a real tough spot," she recalls. "They had to be crackerjack focus-pullers/camera assistants, which they were—we were very lucky. I was operating the camera along with my co-operator, Chris Norr, with whom I worked on **Bamboozled.**"

Working as a team: "On **Eternal** what would happen is we would block the actors on the set in the morning, and then I would figure out how we could put the two cameras in these usually tight spots so that I could get one end of the action and Chris could get the other. For example, if I started out on Jim Carrey, and he crossed the frame, I would let him go across the frame and I would pick up Kate Winslet. And the same thing with Chris—we were always crossing the action, and it became a lot of fun for us, because it was really about the choreography of not only the actors in the scene, but of the cameras. Sometimes we would actually move while the scene was going on, so a lot of the scenes were shot as a one-shot deal with coverage. It was a challenge to shoot, but also very intriguing."

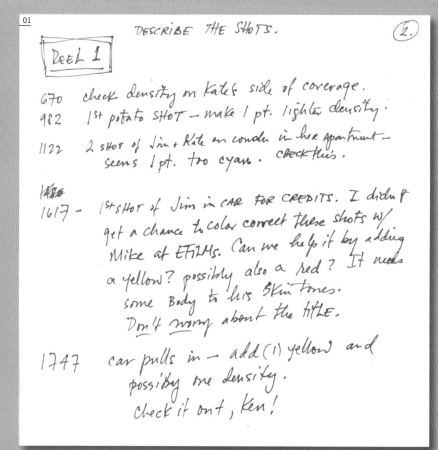

> "If the director starts out by asking me whether or not I'm going to shoot handheld or with a crane or a Steadicam, then I become a bit skeptical about the working relationship."

"You just look at your dailies the next day, and then you make your adjustments." "OK, great, cool." But on **Swoon**, because we didn't have the money to develop negative right away, I didn't see the dailies until three weeks after we finished shooting! I had to go on intuition. To an extent, everybody does.

For me, **Swoon** laid down the first framework of my career: how to do a lot with a little, how to have a plan and be able to change it on the spot, how to be a leader of the crew, and how to collaborate with the director without allowing ego to get in the way. Tom had to trust me because we didn't have a video tap. Sometimes we would shoot one take, and Tom would say, "How was that?" And I would say, "It was amazing, it worked. I could see it working through the camera." And he'd say, "OK, check the gate." To move on after one take was really scary. But it enabled me to trust what I saw through the camera when things worked. It's a hard thing to describe, when it works. There's just a certain kind of symbiosis that happens; the actors know it and can feel it.

We didn't even have a regular dolly, we had a doorway dolly, and the biggest lights I had were two 5k Fresnels. Having very little at hand to make this film also taught me how to take the bare bones of a story and make it work, take the bare bones of lighting and make it work, think about the film in a very spare way so that what comes through is the essence of the story.

When I read a script for the first time, I always take notes in the margin because I'm seeing it in my mind's eye for the first time. When I meet the director, I'm really interested to find out what his or her point of view is. Directors have to convince me of their point of view. It's not that they're interviewing me—a lot of times we're having a conversation about the ideas. I'll ask obliquely, "What do you want to say with this film and how do you want to say it?" If the director starts out by asking me whether or not I'm going to shoot handheld or with a crane or a Steadicam, then I become a bit skeptical about the working relationship. How a film is shot is related to what the director wants to say and is often part of the creative discussion; camera movement is not formulaic in most cases. I also judge a script by the writing and what is possible to achieve within the timeframe and the budget. No matter how large the budget, it is my job as the DP to "make the day." That means that we have to finish the work that was outlined for that particular day, which is not always easy given →

SUMMER OF SAM

(01–02) One of the most creative films that I've made is **Summer of Sam**," says Ellen Kuras. "Spike Lee always encourages me to push the envelope. He once called me a creative muse, and he is definitely one of mine. Spike and I have a fantastic creative relationship and a really strong friendship. I think he's a visionary in so many different ways, but what he brought out in me was to listen to and follow my intuition. This dynamic really emerged and found expression in **Summer of Sam**—I would say to him, 'Spike, I'm thinking about doing this with the light.' And he'd say, 'Good, go for it.' It opened up a whole other visual world where I was allowed to experiment."

"If you're going to work in the film industry—if you're going to be a director, a DP or a producer or anybody—Number 1 Rule is, 'Don't be an asshole.'"

the actors' turnaround schedules and the ever-waning light. I once had to turn down a film on the basis that the budget would not allow me to complete all of the work boarded on the one-liner schedule. I knew that it would've been crazy to think that we could have done night driving shots in the country, rain towers and rain at a different distant location, and underwater shots all in one short night without the right manpower and expertise.

Somebody once asked me, "So, how does it feel having a man's job?" And I said, "I don't have a man's job—I have my own job." Inevitably, the question comes up: "How does it feel to be a woman DP?" I used to get asked this question numerous times, yet I just have to laugh. It's a basic misconception about women leaders in the film industry. What does that mean? Am I different? Well, I am different. Maybe in a good way. I am my own person and I have to create in an individual and unique way. Maybe being a woman helps me to bring a more emotional component to the visual translation. It's never a clear delineation anyway. It's not only about problem-solving, but it's also about "Where is the emotional dimension of the story?" I think that's really important, and sometimes critics forget about that. I prefer to be seen through my work and as a person first.

When it comes to the camera, I want to be very discreet. I know other camerapeople who have to have the biggest dollies—they seem to want to make an announcement when they come on set. I'm always asking for the smallest dollies. Rather than have the camera announce itself, I want it to be a reflection for the actors. I don't want the camera to overpower them. When I'm shooting—and part of this does come from documentary—I try to be very quiet and witness what's happening in the scene while being a participant at the same time. As the camera, I become part of the scene, but in a very discreet way. In **The Ballad of Jack and Rose**, when Jack is alone with his daughter during a very intimate moment, I was lying on the floor, the camera resting against my stomach. Though the camera

movement was strenuous and the silence palpable, I tried with all of my heart to breathe within the pulse of the scene; any breath out of sync would have taken us all out of the moment and thus out of the scene. To me it's really important that I am a participant with the actors—and that I share the same state of mind.

As a director of photography, I direct everything that has to do with photography. Yet, I don't simply see myself as a cinematographer. I'm very embracing and caring of the crew and everything that goes on around me. That means the art department, the wardrobe, everything. Those people are under my wing, and I'm going to take care of them. It's my responsibility.

It's also very important to me that the people that I work with respect each other on and off the set. I tend to work with directors who are respectful toward the crew no matter the size of the movie. The crew is my family. I've worked with the same crew for many, many years. It's so important to treat every person on your set—your PA or whomever—as equally valuable to the making of the project. I find that there's this unspoken hierarchy that becomes more about ego than it does about getting the project done. But it's really important to recognize that any one person is not better than anyone else. I often give talks at universities, and the first thing I'll say to a class is, "If you're going to work in the film industry—if you're going to be a director, a DP or a producer or anybody—Number 1 Rule is, 'Don't be an asshole.'"

BLOW

(01–04) "**Blow** had five different periods. I wanted to make each of the periods feel distinct, but not announce itself to the point where you're saying, 'Oh, we're in the '60s.' It really had to feel transparent to me. I ended up making a book with tear sheets of each period (**01–02**) so I could show director Ted Demme what I was planning to do, and how it was going to look. I thought, 'What lenses do I want to use for that period? What kind of lights do I want to use? What kind of film stock?' So, for example, in the '50s I used old, uncoated-style anamorphic lenses with reversal film, which I processed as reversal, and I used corrected tungsten light. For the '60s, I ended up using tungsten light, but I went to negative. I used very heavy backlight, but yellow backlight—all tungsten again—and I used uncoated amorphic lenses. It creates a different feeling between periods. I was referring to the photography and the movies at the time, and all of that was affected by the film stock available and the lenses available and the kinds of cameras. So when I went to the '70s, I again used uncoated lenses, but I used a magenta filter because what happened with the film stocks in those times is that they would fade and they would have that kind of washed-out magenta feeling to them."

Sven Nykvist

There is no director–cinematographer relationship in the history of cinema that comes close to that between Ingmar Bergman and Sven Nykvist. And no cinematographer created such mesmerizing ties between story and lighting as Nykvist.

He was born in Sweden in 1922 and was already intrigued by photography as a teenager. At the age of 16, he bought a Keystone 8mm camera which he used to film athletes in slow motion doing the high jump. By 19, he was in Stockholm working as an assistant cameraman at Sandrews Studios, and from 1943 to 1945 he moved to Rome to work at Cinecitta. Returning to Sweden in 1945, he got his first cinematographer credit on **The Children From Frostmo Mountain** at the age of 23.

He worked on several Swedish films over the next decade, but his life was to change in 1953 when he was one of three cinematographers on **Sawdust and Tinsel** directed by young hotshot filmmaker Bergman. From then on, Nykvist

became Bergman's sole DP and experimented with lighting to accentuate and enhance the mood in films such as **The Virgin Spring** (1960), **Through a Glass Darkly** (1961) and **Winter Light** (1963).

The black-and-white images in these films are among the most haunting in the era. In **Persona** in 1966, Nykvist went for intense closeups on the actresses Liv Ullmann and Bibi Andersson, daringly fusing the two characters into one. Nykvist said that because Bergman used the same company of actors on most of his films, he was able to study their faces and light every detail.

Ironically, for all the breakthroughs they made together in black and white, Bergman and Nykvist were just as groundbreaking in color, creating a vivid color palette of reds for **Cries and Whispers**, which won Nykvist an Oscar. Mostly shooting on the island of Faro where Bergman lived and worked, Nykvist shot all the films, as well as classic TV series such as **Scenes from a Marriage**, **Face to Face**, and

01

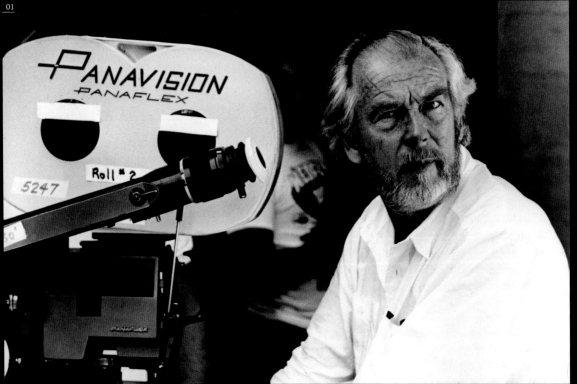

Fanny and Alexander, all of which were reversioned as features. He won a second Oscar for **Fanny and Alexander**.

Nykvist's fame from the Bergman films made him one of the most sought-after cinematographers in the world and he subsequently worked with some of the other great directors. On Roman Polanski's **The Tenant** in 1976, he was encouraged to light the visual detail of each scene often at the expense of the actors— the opposite of Bergman's method. Other collaborators included Louis Malle (**Pretty Baby**, 1978), Bob Fosse (**Star 80**, 1983), Paul Mazursky (**Willie and Phil**, 1980), Jan Troell (**Hurricane**, 1979), Bob Rafelson (**The Postman Always Rings Twice**, 1981), Volker Schlöndorff (**Swann in Love**, 1984), Norman Jewison (**Agnes of God**, 1985), and Philip Kaufman (**The Unbearable Lightness of Being**, 1988).

He was also seen as conduit to the Bergman magic, and worked with filmmakers who admired Bergman such as Andrei Tarkovsky on his final film, **The Sacrifice** (1986), which was shot on the island of Gotland next to Bergman's home island of Faro and starred Bergman's favorite actor, Erland Josephson.

Nykvist also established a rapport with Bergman acolyte Woody Allen, shooting four films including one of Allen's best, **Crimes and Misdemeanors** in 1989. He also shot two films directed by Liv Ullmann—**Kristin Lavransdatter** in 1995 and **Private Confessions** in 1996.

He also directed several films himself, most recently **The Ox** (1991), which featured many of the Bergman regulars including Max von Sydow, Liv Ullmann and Erland Josephson.

He died in 2006 at the age of 83, just under a year before Bergman himself.

02 Face to Face

03 The Serpent's Egg

04 Scenes from a Marriage

05 Autumn Sonata

Peter Suschitzky

"When I look through the camera, I feel as if I am the first person seeing the movie. Now, of course, a director can see a video monitor, but I still feel I am seeing the film for the first time when I look through the camera."

Peter Suschitzky was born in 1941, the son of famed UK cinematographer and photographer Wolfgang Suschitzky whose credits include **Entertaining Mr Sloane** (1970), and **Get Carter** (1971). The younger Suschitzky attended IDEC in Paris at the age of 18 but left the cinematography course after a year to return to London where he became a loader at one of the UK's first commercial studios. From there he moved to become an assistant cameraman on TV documentaries and then, at the age of 21, moved to Latin America where he became lead cameraman on a series of documentaries.

Having seen some of Suschitzky's still photographs, taken while in Latin America, Kevin Brownlow recruited him to be the cinematographer on his ultra-low-budget feature **It Happened Here** (1965). From there, his career moved fast and he shot Peter Watkins' **Privilege** (1967), Albert Finney's directorial debut **Charlie Bubbles** (1967), and Peter Hall's **A Midsummer Night's Dream** (1968). Throughout the 1970s, he worked with renowned directors such as Joseph Losey (**Figures in a Landscape**), John Boorman (**Leo the Last**), Jacques Demy (**The Pied Piper**), and twice with Ken Russell (**Lisztomania**, and **Valentino**). He also shot the legendary musical **The Rocky Horror Picture Show** in 1975 and the box office blockbuster and now classic **The Empire Strikes Back** (1980).

He worked on both sides of the Atlantic in the next two decades, including some high-profile Hollywood titles such as Ulu Grosbard's **Falling in Love**, George Sluizer's remake of **The Vanishing** (1993), Tim Burton's **Mars Attacks!** (1996), and Randall Wallace's star-studded **The Man in the Iron Mask** (1998). But he found his groove as David Cronenberg's cinematographer when he stepped in for Mark Irwin during the pre-production of **Dead Ringers** in 1988. The two have made nine films together since then: **Naked Lunch** (1991), **M. Butterfly** (1991), **Crash** (1996), **eXistenZ** (1999), **Spider** (2002), **A History Of Violence** (2005), **Eastern Promises** (2007), **A Dangerous Method** (2011), and the forthcoming **Cosmopolis** (2012). His son Adam is also a cinematographer, marking the third generation of Suschitzkys behind the camera.

Peter Suschitzky

"" It started when I was a child because my father was a photographer and I would see him working at home in his darkroom. When he closed the door to that room, I just wanted to know what happened in the darkened room with the orange light in it, a room of secrets and promises.

I would knock on the door to be let in and he would sometimes indulge me for a few minutes, but I am sure that I quickly became bored. Eventually he bought me some daylight-designed chemicals and paper after I had been given a Box Brownie camera by a family friend, and I was able to make prints in the garden. At the age of five, I was taking pictures of the family and my father then taught me how to print and develop films. That's how the training of my eye started, and how I became involved in image-making. I started to look at the world and see what would make a good picture.

My first assignment as a cameraman was in Latin America where I spent a year shooting documentaries for German TV. I was only 22 when I shot my first film, **It Happened Here** (1965), and that became my visiting card; I had shot a full-length movie, and it was bought by United Artists when it was completed. We made the film on weekends and I was just able to cope with four small lamps. We had to do some big scenes with these small lamps and we had to carry them around ourselves. Of course we had all seen the influential films of our day such as **Á bout de souffle** (1960), and **Hiroshima Mon Amour** (1959). They influenced us, but I can't say our film looked like a New Wave film and I was only able to do what I could with the modest means at my disposal and with the added ingredient of no experience of movie-making.

For someone so young to be in charge of the photography of a film was unknown in Britain at the time. It was a very hierarchical business and it was the cultural norm to work five to ten years in each job: a loader first, then you would become a focus puller, and then maybe at the age of 35 or

CRASH

(01–03) One of Cronenberg's most influential films was the 1995 film **Crash**, which, Suschitzky says, was "a very tough film to shoot. It was very cold because a percentage of it was outside in the wintertime in Toronto. But the situations written in the script and which the actors had to play out were so extraordinary and inherently funny that I think I laughed more on that film than any other I've worked on. It's very powerful. We had to get inside cars a lot which can be very painful—there is never enough room in a car."

> **"I was probably too anxious about my work in those days to be able to relax and concentrate on the creative aspects of the job."**

40 an operator and then you might get a break as a cinematographer. It was very different then. And everybody wore jackets and ties.

When I did my second film **Privilege** with Peter Watkins, I felt uncomfortable because it seemed as if everybody was looking at me, a youngster, so I had to develop a thick skin. I honestly don't think I was good at what I did until much later and I was probably too anxious about my work in those days to be able to relax and concentrate on the creative aspects of the job.

When I started shooting films, I worked in the traditional manner in the sense that I had a camera operator, but now I prefer to operate myself. When I met Cronenberg, I had already operated myself on a couple of French films, so when he said that the cinematographer he had worked with in the past always operated, I didn't hesitate to say that I preferred that way of working. Retrospectively, I don't like the way one worked in Britain which is the only country that refers to us cinematographers as "lighting cameramen." It's a term I resent deeply because it expresses the way cameramen used to work. The camera operator discussed the camera angles and compositions with the director, and then there was a cameraman who just lit the set. That seems, with hindsight, to be a crazy way of working.

I believe that to become a director of photography one has to have risen through the ranks. Therefore, with all the experience gathered on the way, you will have an opinion about the number of cuts a scene needs, where to put the camera, which lens to use and so on. The director should discuss all these things with the director of photography and not the operator, if there is one. That is, of course, the American way of working and it makes much more sense to do it that way.

I enjoy operating. When I look through the camera, I feel as if I am the first person seeing the movie. Now, of course, a director can see a video monitor but I still feel I am seeing the film for the first time when I look through the camera.

It worked very well between Cronenberg and myself on our first film **Dead Ringers**; on the very first day, things clicked between us and we understood each other straight away. I suggested many ways of shooting the scenes, such as where to put the camera and which lens to use—to think about the next scene and how the editing would work, some of which he had not necessarily given thought to. I urged Cronenberg to use the wide-angle lens, even for closeups on some occasions—it is something I like to use. I prefer to use a wider lens and move the camera when going in for a closeup, rather than just change the lens, and staying put. If you use a telephoto lens, you will emphasize the face, because the background will go soft and you will have a very narrow angle of view. When you use a wider lens and go in close, the audience is still aware of the environment that the actor inhabits. I think the décor, or set, or location says a lot about the character and complements the performance and the text. If you do it all on telephoto lens, you don't see anything, so I have a deep preference for using wider lenses most of the time.

I shot most of **Dead Ringers** on 21mm and 27mm lenses, which is pretty wide. It's much more difficult to do it that way because the director of photography has to take care of the way that the set looks, which entails more work.

The other difference between a telephoto lens and a wide lens is that when a character moves and you are filming on a wide lens, the size of the actor in the frame changes more rapidly. The result is often stronger, but you need to be careful not to look as if one is trying to make a point of it; rather it should still look natural.

Professionally, my relationship with Cronenberg is no longer so verbal. He just lets me get on with my work and we understand each other very quickly. I understand what he wants without saying anything. I seem to remember that for the first film we screened two or three films just to talk about what we liked and didn't like. We don't need to do that anymore. He is very precise about what he wants and very practical and sure of himself in the best of ways, so we don't waste time doing shots that will never →

> "I still feel that I'd rather see a well-written, well-acted, well-directed, but badly photographed film than a well-photographed, but boring film."

be used. I often make suggestions, but he has become more specific than he used to be. Meeting David Cronenberg was the most fortunate professional meeting of my life. I know that I am lucky to be able to work with such a good filmmaker who is somebody I like immensely as well.

When I watch a film, I want to be absorbed in the narrative of the film just like anyone else. It's only when I get bored that I start to notice the cinematography. I still feel that I'd rather see a well-written, well-acted, well-directed, but badly photographed film than a well-photographed, but boring film. I still feel very strongly that the script

is the first important thing; I have sometimes seen a good script turned into a bad film but I have never seen a bad script become a good film. The script is the skeleton on which the body of the film must hang.

I hope that I respond to what I feel that the story needs in visual terms. I like to talk about the design, depending on the director I am working with. The preparation of the film and the choice of the locations often takes place before I get there, as I am usually working far from home.

Something to bear in mind about Cronenberg is that he always resists illustration in film. He will never allow a shot to stay in the edit (and →

THE EMPIRE STRIKES BACK

(01–03) George Lucas had Suschitzky in mind to shoot **Star Wars**, reputedly because he was a fan of his work on Peter Watkins' **Privilege** which he had seen when he was a student. The two met at the 20th Century Fox offices in London. "The first thing I said to him, quite foolishly, but honestly, was that he didn't really want me because I had no experience with special effects," he recalls. "I suggested Geoffrey Unsworth who shot **2001**, but Lucas said he was unavailable. Fox recognized that what I said was correct and that I didn't have the qualifications for a film with a relatively inexperienced director and on that scale."

Lucas came back to Suschitzky for the sequel **The Empire Strikes Back** after **Star Wars** had become the biggest box office hit of all time. "I was called in to meet the director Irvin Kershner who was a great character and very likeable," says Suschitzky.

Having secured the job, Suschitzky went out to Lucasfilm headquarters in northern California. "We sat down at this big table with lots of people around it who were going to be working on the special effects. We had a storyboard in front of us and I noticed that when the questions came up about how we were going to do this or that, everybody looked at each other. Nobody knew. I realized it was going to be a process of exploration."

He learned fast how to shoot blue screen and front projection and says that he was helped by the shooting time of six months and the presence on set of special-

effects supervisors. By the production's end, however, Suschitzky was asked to solve a key problem. The art department had run out of budget so could only hang black drapes in the carbon freezing chamber where Luke Skywalker and Darth Vader would face each other for the film's final duel. "We came up with the idea of filling the stage with smoke and steam and filling it with lights to hide the drapes," he says. "It worked well."

01

Dealing with reflections

Darth Vader, says Suschitzky, provided "plenty of interesting problems of reflection." "You could see yourself and the lamps reflected in the helmet and in those days it was much harder to do post-production work to get rid of embarrassing reflections. So I had to learn how to handle that. I had to put up objects or panels on the set behind the camera that would reflect in an interesting way on the helmet or the body armor."

he doesn't usually allow a shot to be filmed) if it is pure illustration or because it might look striking. On **Eastern Promises**, we had a scene in a very tough location, one of the most difficult I've ever had to tackle: it was an alleyway with high walls on either side at night and it was very hard to find a place to put the light. At the end of the alleyway was the River Thames, so it was also physically very difficult, cold, and windy. We shot on that location during the day and at night, and I suggested that it would be good to do a pan looking down the Thames onto the alleyway and he said "No, it will never be in the film. It takes up too much time in the edit and I will never use it." So we didn't shoot it. I just thought the Thames looked very striking, but he will never put a shot in just because it's pretty.

I don't like storyboarding. I can see that it's very useful for an action film or special-effects sequences because you can sit down with the stunt coordinators or special-effects people and work out how you are going to do a scene. Otherwise I think it's an instrument that can imprison and limit the imagination, because if you storyboard the whole film, it's very difficult to imagine how to shoot it in a different manner than that shown on the storyboard.

When you come to shoot a film, ideally you should leave space for what inspires you on the day. The actors and locations are going to tell you that different things are needed and it's very difficult to escape the images that you already have in your mind from a storyboard.

On **Mars Attacks!**, everything was storyboarded and Tim Burton spent time and money filming the storyboard and cutting it so that he had a sense of the rhythm of the story and the whole film. Then he never looked at them again. That's the ideal. Put them aside and don't bring them to the set.

I do a certain amount of preparation, looking at locations with the director and technical team, but I work very instinctively. I know that I have to discuss with the gaffer roughly where we are going to put the lights, but I never know exactly what I am going to do until I do it. I leave a lot of space in my head to react to the first rehearsal on set.

I love actors and I understand their vulnerability. I have heard some Directors of Photography say that it's all about the acting, but I don't think so: I think everything has to come together. My idea of a really fine film is when the style and content come together and I don't think you should leave it all to the actors to do exactly as they like because, like all people, they need to be given limits. If you can suggest that they would look better standing in one place talking rather than wandering off to the corner of the room, then you should tell them. I am not against giving actors marks, but I have heard that some directors hate it. →

01–02 Peter Suschitzky and David Cronenberg on the set of **A Dangerous Method**

NAKED LUNCH

(01–03) David Cronenberg's brilliant film of William S. Burroughs' **Naked Lunch** presented Suschitzky with numerous challenges, not least of which was the fact that the entire section of the film set in the fictional North African province of "Interzone" would have to be shot in a studio. "We were going to shoot part of them in Morocco but the Gulf War broke out," he says. "Before we started shooting, I suggested that we build expressionist-style sets because the material was so strange, but he said that he wanted it to be rooted in reality. Still, I put everything I felt about expressionism into my lighting."

All the African exteriors were therefore shot on a sound stage in Toronto. "For that you need quite a lot of light. In the market scenes, I had some of the light coming from above through slats and nets to give a dappled effect. There was also a street scene where the actors went up steps and narrow streets, which was tough to light."

Suschitzky particularly enjoyed lighting the scenes in Burroughs' Interzone apartment in which he has a constant dialogue with a talking typewriter and its anus. "It was all special effects done on the stage in front of the camera and I had never filmed a talking arsehole before. Of course I had met plenty in the course of a long film career," he laughs. "I wanted a very expressive lighting style in that apartment. I wanted to have interest and mystery in it. So it's got lots of shadows in it and to do that isn't simple and quite labor-intensive. I used a lot of flags. Quite often it was difficult to get into the set because there were so many flags."

"Nobody has explained to me what the virtues of handheld are. First of all it makes me sick to watch it. I get motion sickness and I resent that when I go to the cinema."

I am very sensitive to actors' performances. If I see what I think is a second-rate performance, I get very upset because I want the whole film to be excellent. I feel very attached to, and involved in, the filmmaking process and I am sensitive to the dramatic needs of the scene. The attitude in general to camerawork and actors has changed a lot during my lifetime. They used to say to the director of photography that you had to see the actors all the time, and many producers would be upset if the actors were in shadows. That's where the money is, they used to say. But I don't feel it's necessary to see the actors all the time. A character is built up like a puzzle, and once you have seen an actor a few times, you know what they look like, even if they are in shadow. That sounds commonplace, but it didn't used to be.

I am not, on the whole, in favor of handheld camera unless it involves a scene where a character is running or something similar. I don't like to be aware of the camera wobbling. Nobody has explained to me what the virtues of handheld are. First of all it makes me sick to watch it, and I resent that when I go to the cinema. I have a theory that directors who like handheld work think that it's more real. Why do they think that it's more real? Perhaps because it's more like a home movie. But my argument against it is that if you walk down the street without a camera, you have a Steadicam in your brain and the image you are seeing is totally smooth. So it's not closer to reality, it's just closer to home movies. I hate it, it's imprecise.

I don't like the idea of shooting a whole film on Steadicam either. I like Steadicam when the camera has to go up some stairs, or along a street, or across a field—somewhere where you cannot satisfactorily build a track. But I am against shooting a whole film on Steadicam because the framing is never going to be precise —it is always approximate in framing, and on static shots it breathes with the operator and is distracting.

THE ROCKY HORROR PICTURE SHOW
(01–02) Suschitzky has only shot one musical but it happened to be one of the most famous of them all. "Our budget was $250,000 and that was low," he recalls. "It was shot in England in six weeks and shooting a musical in six weeks is very demanding. We had to do it in a very simple way. I remember at the time thinking that the dance numbers needed more cuts, more angles, but we just didn't have the time to give it the attention. I didn't understand or appreciate how wonderful it was at the time."

The post-production process is very interesting to me. It can be very creative in the best of circumstances. Most films are digitized, of course, now. I go to the laboratory or post-production facility when the film has been cut and almost finished and I will do my post-production timing. In the UK it's called grading. I sit with a technician in front of a screen and perform what is essentially a giant version of Photoshop. I have a lazer pointer and I will point to the top of the screen and ask to make the top of the image darker or take some red or blue or green out. One can do very subtle things. You can darken a specific area or lighten it or you can change the overall color or the brightness and density of the image. You can make one side of an actor's face darker than the other, if you want. You can emphasize things.

I don't seek to change my work radically in post. I still aim to get everything as correct as possible to my eye in front of the camera while we are filming, and I want it to look filmic and not manipulated. But I can enhance my work, and make it look a bit better in post. It takes between one and two weeks to do, and after that my role on the film is finished.

I still want to do films with other directors but I am very picky now. I only get to choose from what I am offered, but I only want to work on films with a good script that I like the sound of. And with people I like.

I look back on the films I've shot and think, "Oh God, I wish I'd done it better." I am still full of self-doubt. Perhaps that's not a bad thing. ,,

Seamus McGarvey

"Something happens when you look through glass…Things are slightly at odds or askew in a cinema frame. That's how it should be, because we want to see things in poetic translation, as if through a type of gauze."

Born in Northern Ireland, Seamus McGarvey began his career as a stills photographer before attending film school at the University of Westminster in London. On graduating in 1988, he began shooting short films, documentaries and music videos for the likes of U2, Paul McCartney, and The Rolling Stones.

McGarvey's first feature was Michael Winterbottom's debut film **Butterfly Kiss** in 1995, and he quickly gained a name for features such as Alan Rickman's directorial debut **The Winter Guest** (1997) starring Emma Thompson, and Tim Roth's **The War Zone** (1999). His first US feature was **High Fidelity** in 2000 with director Stephen Frears, and since then he has worked with an impressive range of filmmakers such as Mike Nichols (**Wit**, 2001), Michael Apted (**Enigma**, 2001), Stephen Daldry (**The Hours**, 2002), Oliver Stone (**World Trade Center**, 2006), Anthony Minghella (the pilot for TV series **The No. 1 Ladies' Detective Agency**, 2008), and Joe Wright on both **The Soloist** (2009), and **Atonement** (2007), for which he was nominated for an Oscar and a BAFTA. His mainstream Hollywood credits include **Along Came Polly** (2004), **Sahara** (2005), and **Charlotte's Web** (2006). His most recent features are Lynne Ramsay's **We Need to Talk About Kevin** (2011), and the epic Marvel comic-book movie **The Avengers** (2012), directed by Joss Whedon.

Seamus McGarvey

" I am always trepidatious around the camera and in awe of it, because I see it as a little sleeping dragon. Something alchemical happens with a camera and it becomes like a receptor for different atmospheres and vibes around the set. It becomes a portal through which everyone's ideas pass from the director, and production designer to the producer, who might be in tune photographically or not. A camera and a lens are not inanimate objects: lenses in particular have personalities and histories.

Something happens when you look through glass. The idea when you look through a lens is that you are telescoping things or expanding things. Things are attenuated or distorted through a lens. Nothing is real. That happens particularly with anamorphic lenses, because you are effectively concertina-ing up the real world and then expanding it again. In that process, things are pulled or bent out of shape and that's the beauty of it because what you see is not what you recognize as real. Things are slightly at odds or askew in a cinema frame. And that's how it should be, because we want to see things in poetic translation, as if through a type of gauze.

The first time I watched a movie and noticed the cinematography was during what is still my favorite movie, **A Matter of Life and Death** (1946). I actually watched it on a black-and-white TV, and for years I thought the film was in black and white! But then when I watched it again, I suddenly saw that the earth was in vivid Technicolor! I became a great friend of Jack Cardiff's and he was a mentor to me. He was the greatest cinematographer, in my view. He took on Technicolor and basically tortured the stock and the process with his unique artist's eye to make these great images. He did everything you were supposed not to do. A gentleman maverick. He basically plugged in his cinematographic guitar and fuzzbox and off he went to change cinema!

It's interesting because cinematography is about both craft and technique. I see it

THE HOURS

(01–02) **The Hours** is a three-part film with each segment set in a different time period, but McGarvey and director Stephen Daldry worked to link each segment. "We mirrored camera moves and framings between the three just so there was a sense of history repeating itself and stories superimposing through the eras." McGarvey used three different kinds of film stock for the three periods. "For the Virginia Woolf section, I wanted a tobacco/nicotine feel and something that had a richness of the 1920s. For the 1950s section we talked about a wan, draining away of life so we went for a very pale, low-contrast stock that Kodak made at the time." He also played with exposure to create a lower contrast, and employed the bleach bypass process which reduces the color and increases grain.

unequivocally as an art and every time we look through a camera, we have to remember that word "Art" and to see from the heart. I hope that we all remember what effectively moves us, especially when the commerce and the business of it all is to the forefront. For instance, you look at Tarkovsky and other people who were working on a grand scale, but their films are absolutely soaked in vision and personal art. There really is space for that approach, even in mainstream cinema, because I think those things are beyond language and that is a great thing for cinema. They can communicate profound universal notions through images, even in silence.

Part of that is in the casting. Frears used to say that if he picked the right person, his job was done, and of course he would grapple with so much else, but in a sense he's right. And Tarkovsky knew this too. He picked people who had a look or an atmosphere about them and put them through their paces around a set. So it's a great set, a great face. It's puppeteering, effectively, and that is very often wordless. You see wordless drama happening with incredibly emotionless faces that are expressive in their movement. Then they are operated by humans on a set with a little bit of music and dramatic lighting. It's filmmaking 101, really!

Visually you have to set your terms in the opening frames. You see the first few frames of **The Double Life of Veronique**, for example, and it's all yellow and you are sitting in the cinema and thinking something's gone wrong with the projector. But after a while you realize they meant to do that and suddenly you are lured into this world, you are *sutured*, as the French would say. It's about stitching an audience into your vision and, once you've selected your terms, you abandon all reality. Then as an audience you are effectively at sea in the filmmaker's world: You surrender.

I think that the danger with digital filmmaking, and the idea of "we'll fix it in post" is that the vision and intent can go out of the window. Everything's possible after the event, but after the event, it will almost certainly be a coterie of →

01–02 Seamus McGarvey on the set of Sam Taylor Wood's **Nowhere Boy** (2009)

> "Simplicity is always good because inevitably on a film you do get multifarious voices and too many cooks spoil the broth."

people who will inform the look of the film: It's cinematography by committee. I have always found that something magical happens on a set. There is an energy, focus, direction, and respect. Something special happens there and then on the set and if you can capture it, it is undeniably a stronger cinema experience.

Simplicity is always good because inevitably on a film you do get multifarious voices and too many cooks spoil the broth. If you can reduce that, there is a clearer message, and you can hear the singular voice of the filmmaker. It's like somebody singing in the forest. It sounds and looks like cinema. That's what I mean by seeing by one's heart. The picture goes from eye to heart to screen without the brain consciously intercepting—instinct plays a huge role. I think filmmakers, in danger of this outside influence, have got to circle their wagons. The film set is a special zone, a sacred arena, and it needs to be protected.

I don't think you have to be pathologically happy on every film you do and I don't think it necessarily produces the greatest work when everything is running smoothly. There has to be a tension and electricity, and a familial atmosphere can very often become too homely and plump. On **High Fidelity**, for example, Stephen Frears felt that the air was going out of the set whenever things were going well and he would throw a "hand grenade" into situations in order to destabilize them. Oliver Stone is the same. He likes to stir the pot in a kind of mischievous way, and I like that because it produces unexpected results. Somehow it adrenalizes the proceedings.

When I meet a director, I tend not to do a whole song and dance number because sometimes that overwhelms them. The director will usually have been working on a project for perhaps years and has clear notions of what they want. I do have clear ideas when I read a script, because every script has photographic signatures and a cinematographic heart to it when you read it. It always provokes visual ideas. So I will have those ideas and I will have noted them down or they will be in the back of my head.

However, I like to get a sense of how the director is imagining the film before I offer my thoughts.

Every director is different and I am a different cinematographer with each director. Joe Wright was very precise about **Atonement**. Before production, we just sat down and worked through the script scene by scene and did little stick-insect storyboards, discussed the arc of the film, and talked very specifically about shots. It was like a paper edit of the film so we could find our rhythm and the look and feel. There was hardly a shot in the film that wasn't planned out months in advance. I liked working like that because it gave Joe more time on the set to work with the actors and it allowed me more time to light. We knew exactly what we were going for in everything from color to lighting style and camera movement.

Actually for all that precision, there was a lot of liquidity and elasticity in our approach as well. Within that safe structure, there was a lot of space for improvisation on the fly, so a lot happened on the day. There were aspects of that film that were extremely carefully planned, but at the same time, we were able to react to moments that happened, particularly in terms of weather or nature. I mean that's when it really came into its own, when you can look at little motes of dust flying through the air and get the actor to run through them. Or the archway of flowers we tracked through on Steadicam. Those were all shots we came up with in the moment.

I love mixing and matching projects. I am about to begin shooting on this epic superhero movie, **The Avengers**, and I have just finished the sort of film I would normally do, which is Lynne Ramsay's **We Need to Talk About Kevin**. Both have extremely different photographic approaches. It's almost like they are different art forms, but I think that's really interesting; it sort of throws you around a bit. I hate to approach every film with a formula because it stops you thinking creatively.

We shot **We Need to Talk About Kevin** in anamorphic 35mm, but it's incredibly stark and static. Lynne wanted a different look for this film. We pushed people to the edges and used →

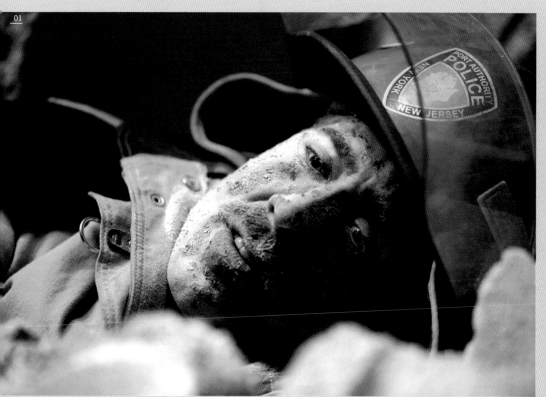

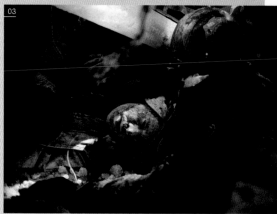

WORLD TRADE CENTER

(01–03) Although McGarvey said it was nerve-racking stepping into the shoes of Stone's long-time cinematographer Robert Richardson on **World Trade Center**, he felt that the film had to be shot without the bombastic approach that sometimes characterizes Stone's work. "I felt it had to be something simpler and plainer and more respectful in a way. Sometimes Oliver would tease me about the conservatism in my photographic approach, but most of the movie is quite static. The first 20 minutes [the set-up before the Twin Towers fall] is kind of kinetic. We establish the characters going to work and we produced an ebullience in that, a sense of the diurnal routine. The camera necessarily had a rat-a-tat rhythm to it and it was sort of chaotic in a way, because we knew that as soon as they were inside this hole, this rubble, it was going to be fixed, a stasis. And darkness."

Production designer Jan Roelfs built a huge replica of the WTC lobby and the rubble of the two towers and the hole in which the two protagonists were stuck. McGarvey says it was the biggest set he's ever shot, but because of the dust and dripping water it was "a terrifying set to work on and hugely uncomfortable. It was a horror for us and the camera."

"We looked at films such as **A Man Escaped** (1956) in terms of exploring a constriction, but opening it up for an audience," says McGarvey. "We explored the psychological space with the camera through the use of a wide-angle lens. Oliver kept encouraging me to go darker and darker and the studio was freaking out and at a certain point I told him 'Look, Oliver, we're going to go through a Digital Intermediate afterwards and we can pull it down further but still have details there if you want it.' I've seen it since and you can hear the dialogue but you can barely see anything."

ATONEMENT

(01–06) The first section of the three-act film takes place on the hottest day of the year in summer 1939. To ensure the effect of hot, burning sun, McGarvey said he needed a heavy filter to retain consistency through all the lighting set-ups. "We used Christian Dior 10-denier stockings stretched on the back of the lens," he laughs. "It's an old Hollywood technique and all cinematographers used to use it to give their leading ladies a kind of Garbo glow."

For the third section of the film **(02)**, which, it emerges, is a fantasy, McGarvey used another filter. "We played with light in the windows, just to lend things a kind of spectral feel. Skin tones have a kind of wan, opalescent look to them. We wanted the skin tones to look like alabaster."

05

ATONEMENT
SHOT LIST
DAY 57
TUESDAY 22ND AUGUST

SC 115/116: EXT. BRAY DUNES, DAY.

1) 4'30" STEADICAM shot moving through the entire set.
   Starting on Mule tracking vehicle parallel with
   Robbie, Mace, Nettle and Naval officer, play dialogue.
   Move through burning vehicle to line of horses being
   shot. Move round back of boat (for my Mum) and pass
   bonfire with burning Bible pages wiping f/g. Pan up to
   sails of boat, wind machine inside hull of boat. Cross
   the beach to gun placement where we find crying
   soldier. Reveal bandstand. Move round choir on
   bandstand in opposite direction to Mace. Steadicam
   mounts rickshaw. Move back down centre of street with
   big wheel centre frame and stunt men hanging off it.
   Circus horses appear from around corner and gallop in
   opposite direction to camera. Use round-about to bring
   camera L-R. Pass under barrel of guns past trucks
   having their radiators shot out. Finally pan Robbie,
   Nettle and Mace on to pier and follow over shoulder
   until they enter bar. Then pan round to reveal WS of
   beach and continue to end of scaffold pier to reveal
   steel works between boat and bandstand.

GOOD LUCK PETE, GOOD LUCK TEAM!

The five-and-a-half-minute tracking shot

The problems with the beach shoot: The film became famous, or in some camps infamous, for a daring five-and-a-half-minute tracking shot on the beaches of Dunkerque in 1940 (**05–06**). McGarvey said that Wright came up with the idea. "When he mentioned it, I was very wary of it. We had been going to the location and the tide was coming in and the light was bad for most of the day. I was struggling with Joe trying to work out which way we were going to shoot. We could only shoot in one direction because the art department could only afford to shoot in one direction. We had several different little scenes, seven pages of dialogue, to shoot over three days. But when we worked out our time windows of light, it only gave us two hours a day. So Joe just said 'Let's devise a shot and do it in one.' I was resistant because I didn't want to do something show-offy at that point in the film, because the character of Robbie was disintegrating at this point. I felt the whole thing was unnecessarily operatic and at odds with what we were trying to do photographically at that stage in the movie."

Creating the feel and solving the light: Although he initially argued against it, McGarvey was won round, especially when he realized that one shot could give him the light he needed. "Joe argued that the spinning fairground wooziness of Steadicam, which was the only way to shoot it on the beach, could be incredibly appropriate and if we added incidental dreamscapes and discordant images, it would lend the shot a hallucinatory feel."

Making it work: Wright and McGarvey did three takes of the scene—which was all the time they had before the sun went down. "There are dissonant moments and lots of mistakes, but they did very little CGI on it," he says. "The art department had spent so much money building that set and it was such a hugely brave thing for production to do. I remember taking the 400-feet roll of film and saying to the loader. 'This is the magazine. This is the most expensive roll you'll ever load.'"

negative space so there's almost this electricity in the nothingness. Lynne Ramsay started out as a cinematographer herself and her style is so cinematic. She knows how to point a camera at a story and tell it not with words but with a lens. This was also the first time I used a digital camera alongside the film camera on a feature film; I used a Canon EOS 5D MkII. I shot really intimate flashback scenes of Eva (played by Tilda Swinton) and Franklin (John C. Reilly) making love in very low light. Literally the whole scene was illuminated by a flashing neon light outside the window—there was no other lighting in the room. We did a little preshoot to test the camera out. We put Tilda and John in costume and went out in New York on a rainy night. We filmed them with available light in the street and actually it's the most beautiful footage I've ever shot in my life! There was just me, the director, and the actors and there was a strange intimacy to it. The camera allowed for ad hoc, true moments—little movements that would never have been possible

to capture using a big film camera. I got very excited by it as it reminded me of the dynamism and momentum of Derek Jarman's sets when we used to charge around with our Super 8 cameras.

We are shooting **The Avengers** in 3D and that is another string to the cinematographer's bow. I think it's really interesting to me that these characters are larger than life anyway and I can play with their form and their scale just by adjusting the intra-ocular distance and convergence and the position of the screen in a room. I'm anticipating that we'll be working with the choreography of actors in the frame to make use of that spatial relationship, rather than creating depth with lens changes or cutting between long lenses and wide-angle lenses. In 2D cinema, that's what creates a sense of depth and ways of exploring space. I like the idea of returning to a more innocent approach where actors move in a frame and then you let the action run. I think there's enough in those shifts in shape and form and space to keep an

THE WAR ZONE

(01–02) McGarvey jokes that Tim Roth's bleak directorial debut **The War Zone** was "a symphony of gray and cyan, but that was the look we were going for." "It was about distance between people and the spaces inside the frame, but it was also about contrast and darkness," he explains. "The children in the film hadn't acted before and they were like fireflies darting across the set. So between Tim and me, we would try to streamline the blocking and once he was comfortable with the performance we would move in and get it right. But sometimes we didn't actually rehearse and Tim would tell me to stick the camera there on one lens and follow the actors like wildlife photography. We did that a few times and some of the most powerful moments in the film were shot like that. We went very Ken Loach on it and there were no lights in the frame."

> ## "Learning about 3D has been like a kindergarten for me. It's like I am re-learning cinema."

audience engaged, even an audience used to staccato cutting. I think that we're going to play with depth behind the screen in this film and only occasionally adjust the convergence. 3D is tailor-made for a comic-book type of movie, although I can still be gentle with it and use it at specific times. I don't want to overuse that 3D effect.

Learning about 3D has been like a kindergarten for me. It's like I am re-learning cinema. It's literally a different perspective because I'm shooting digitally in stereo but it's also a very big budget studio film so there is a nervousness and energy that I am getting a charge from. I'm translating it from anxiety into creative energy. I hope! **"**

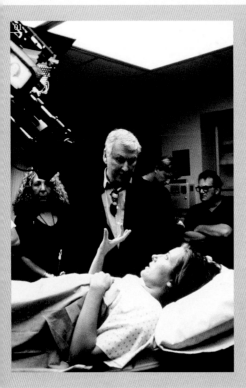

WIT

(01–02) McGarvey teamed up with actress Emma Thompson with whom he had worked on **The Winter Guest** (1997) and famed director Mike Nichols on **Wit** (2001), the film of Margaret Edson's harrowing play which was made for US pay-TV network HBO. Shot on 35mm, the drama mainly took place in a hospital of which a large set was created with lighting built into it. "It was the first time I had worked on that kind of a set and it was great because I could light the hospital and all I needed to add was a little Kino Flo or Chinese lantern.

"We had a starkness and unfiltered look for the hospital interiors and used a different kind of light system for the flashbacks, like swinging tilt lenses, so we could affect focus and shift the plane of focus. That means that the lens was effectively on a bellows. Also I warmed the film up for the flashbacks, using quite warm antique suede filters."

Javier Aguirresarobe

"I don't like to hear spectators say my cinematography was fantastic but the movie was not very good. The best cinematography is when it doesn't have to be one of the protagonists of the film."

One of Spain's leading cinematographers, Javier Aguirresarobe, began his career in the early 1970s shooting shorts and documentaries. Since then, he has gone on to be nominated for 11 Goyas—the Spanish equivalent of the Academy Awards—and has won six times.

It was his work with writer–director Alejandro Amenábar on **The Others** (2001) and **The Sea Inside** (2004) that introduced him to worldwide audiences, who were immediately enraptured by his deeply atmospheric, yet still naturalistic images. Besides working with Pedro Almodóvar on **Talk to Her** (2002), he has also shot films for Woody Allen (**Vicky Cristina Barcelona**, 2008), James Ivory (**The City of Your Final Destination**, 2009), and John Hillcoat (**The Road**, 2009). Depending on the project, Aguirresarobe is quite capable of conjuring a world of romantic warmth or lingering unease, but no matter the assignment he insists on creating a realistic lighting design that emphasizes natural light as much as possible. Recently, he was the DP for the lucrative Twilight franchise, shooting **New Moon** (2009) and **Eclipse** (2010).

Javier Aguirresarobe

❝ I had an older brother who was a still photographer, so since I was very young I was helping out with developing images. The smells of chemicals were already kind of ingrained in me, and by the time I was 16 or 17 I was already doing professional stills photography work.

When I was 18, I was inspired by seeing a film by Carlos Saura called **La Caza** (1966). I was in Madrid at the time but not yet in film school, but as soon as I saw that film, I immediately felt the pull. We've all had fantasies as children about what we wanted to be, but when I saw that, I knew I wanted to be in film. **La Caza** was in black and white and was shot by Luis Cuadrado, a Spanish cinematographer. He managed to create such a complete atmosphere with the photography, that the spectator couldn't help but feel the exact environment in which this film was happening. I felt the heat, I felt the atmosphere, but I also realized that this wasn't just a cold piece of art to admire—it's a craft that can transmit a full range of emotions. I couldn't join film school until I was 20, so I was just preparing myself with other studies to be ready for that.

I learned the craft of filmmaking in school, but nobody can really teach you the actual photographic interpretation of a story. That comes from your own personal experiences— only that will tell you what the cinematographic style should be for any given story. The technique and the craft you learn in school are key to being able to solve any problems later on the set, but the technique itself should not be a heavy weight on your shoulders. It should stay in the back of your mind so you can concentrate on the creative side of things.

When I went to work on **The Others**, I thought about **La Caza**, because they both had certain limitations that they were supposed to work within. I wanted to do the exact opposite of what was the typical lighting formula of a horror movie—those ideas had become clichés that merely helped people enjoy the process of watching the film, as opposed to making them

VICKY CRISTINA BARCELONA

(01–03) While some might assume that Aguirresarobe's work on effects-driven movies such as **New Moon** or **Eclipse** would be the most demanding, he instead points to **Vicky Cristina Barcelona**. "Some of the interior scenes I shot were extremely complicated," he says. "You might not notice it, but it was quite difficult to accomplish just because they're continuous shots and you had to figure out a way to hide all of the lights and to be able to see the whole room. Photography is really not complicated on a huge set on a street with huge lights everywhere. What's difficult is shooting in a very reduced space, where actually things are happening to the characters and you need to be able to see their eyes and their expressions and feel that what's happening is real." **(01)** Aguirresarobe with Woody Allen on the set of **Vicky Cristina Barcelona**.

> "I have the utmost respect for the art of natural light, and I try to stay as truthful to it as I can. I like a certain amount of order in the light direction."

afraid. That's not what I wanted to do. I was recalling my own fears in certain situations—moments and places in my own home when I've felt fearful. I felt that a more naturalistic approach was scarier than faking something that wouldn't be real or that you couldn't relate to. I hoped that the spectator would identify with the characters and feel that they were within the story—I wanted them to feel like it could be him or her right there, as opposed to just being outside looking in.

In general, my lighting is based on how the space feels in the specific location or situation, how the relationship of the space feels. I have the utmost respect for the art of natural light and I try to stay as truthful to it as I can. I like a certain amount of order in the light direction—I don't like light coming from everywhere. Color-wise, I don't like using many colors. The spectator might not know how, technically, films get made, but they're fully aware of what a film is. To be a good filmmaker, the spectator needs to feel pulled in and engaged with the film. I don't like

to hear spectators say my cinematography was fantastic but the movie was not very good. For me, the biggest compliment I can get is when a spectator says, "I didn't notice the cinematography." The best cinematography is when it doesn't have to be one of the protagonists of the film.

A huge reason why **The Others** was so successful is not only because of the cinematography—it's that the script itself was so strong and so well put together. I was given the script initially, but it took them a whole year before they could start shooting because they were considering Nicole Kidman and she was at that moment busy with **Moulin Rouge!**. Then **The Sixth Sense** came up, and everybody was afraid because of story similarities. But in the year that went by, the script didn't change by the time we started shooting.

For me, a script is like an imaginative screen to begin visualizing the film. It allows me to start envisioning the type of texture, the type of color palette, and the atmosphere I'm going to give →

> "I know that most of the time I'll have really good people leading the other departments. That gives me a little more freedom to take some risks."

to it. It's mostly in my head, but then when I start location scouting, I begin imagining the imaginary with the real space. Ultimately, it just happens—or at least it happens to me—that most times when I start filming I begin seeing what I had envisioned.

With **The Others**, this was the first time I worked with an actress of the caliber of Nicole Kidman, so I wanted to make sure she would always look fantastic. So in that sense, I consider myself to be a classic-style cinematographer because I truly believe that the actors and actresses should look fantastic, especially for the audience. Even though the movie might call for certain risks about the way things might look, the actor or the actress needs to look great.

When I make a film in Spain, I do two different types of work—one is a creative and artistic side of what the cinematographer should do with the narrative storytelling, but I also have to be a gaffer type of person. I need to be a little more hands-on giving orders as to what tools and what lights need to be used. In America, the gaffer actually takes on a little more of that work, which frees me up and makes me feel much more protected. I feel quite sheltered in big Hollywood productions because I know that most of the time I'll have really good people leading the other departments. That gives me a little more freedom to take some risks.

I've also noticed that in American filmmaking there's constant meetings, meetings, meetings. This is not the way that films are made in Spain. The tendency to have meetings has advantages and disadvantages. The advantage is that everybody at the end of a meeting has come to a clear idea of how everybody's going to solve any particular issue, but the disadvantage to that is that they marry you to that. There might be a different or better solution down the road, but it's very difficult to change that afterwards. I value very much the ability to allow the moment to dictate what decision should be made. That's why it's hard to predetermine how you're going to light any given scene a week from now. There's a certain number of elements that just happen on

the day or the moment, and I want to put them into play.

With Woody Allen, there are no meetings to be had. He moves fast, and he's actually capable of changing something or improvising in the moment. He is not a man of many words—he knows what he wants to see on the screen, and that's his guiding principle. With **Vicky Cristina Barcelona**, the only condition was to make a warm movie. To prepare, I went back and saw pretty much all of Woody Allen's films. I felt **Husbands and Wives** (1992) was quite a similar movie to this one, so I really studied that film particularly to see what kind of stylistic choices Woody Allen was making. So, we had almost an unspoken collaboration—I would suggest what I thought would be to his liking, and Woody Allen went, "Yeah, great." It was absolute trust.

But it was a very, very difficult movie—if not the most difficult movie—for me to work on, because with Woody Allen there are no monitors. He just stands behind the camera looking at the actors—that's the way he directs. And he pretty much shoots rehearsals, so there's really no rehearsal. Plus the process in post is quite classic—there's no Digital Intermediate. So because the shots were quite long, and the actors were moving throughout the space, I knew I was not going to have the chance of correcting any of this in DI. I had to keep adjusting, moving the T-stop constantly while we were filming. And Woody doesn't do the traditional type of covering a scene—he would ask me to pan from one actor to the other, but to pan when they're not talking versus when they're talking. Because it's not conventional, it's like a breath of fresh air. That's his style and that's why he's one of the greatest directors there is—there's no young director who directs the way that he does.

Every film has its challenges. With **The Sea Inside**, it needed to be as truthful as possible. Although it might sound quite absurd, an important thing for me to accomplish with the lighting was that it created a sense of the smell of the ocean that Javier Bardem's character might have inside his bedroom. And although →

THE OTHERS

(01–03) "For **The Others**, a key element of the atmosphere was either creating smoke or using exterior locations that had a combination of natural fog plus created smoke." When it came to the film's lighting, though, Aguirresarobe quickly discovered a major obstacle. "I couldn't really hang any lighting off the walls because we always had the ceilings in the frame," he recalls, "so I was constantly moving the light as we were filming. The electricians were actually moving with the camera, hiding behind curtains—they would be on the floor, and as soon as Nicole Kidman walked by them, they would get up. By the time she turned around, they were back on the floor." (03) Javier Aguirresarobe, Nicole Kidman, and crew.

Filming a running scene

He also incorporated a trick during a challenging scene that takes place outside of the film's haunted house. "There's a scene where Nicole Kidman runs to her husband, which was created on a stage. She's running 70 or 80 meters very fast, and the camera is dollying around and coming behind her. That's when you start feeling that something's coming toward her and you don't really know what it is. Once the camera comes behind her, we can see the husband coming from a distance toward her. There really isn't a stage that would have enough size to film that, so we actually put her on a kind of treadmill. She's walking on the treadmill, but she's not really moving—it's the camera that's moving. I've actually done this trick several times because—with the smoke, you don't notice it."

> "I'm a little superstitious—if there's a task on a film that I think is quite impossible, and all of a sudden it works out, then I truly believe that the movie is going to be a great movie."

creating that sense of a smell is really not possible, for me it was a guiding light. When I was looking through the eyepiece at Bardem's room, I needed to feel that this house was right next to the ocean. If I didn't feel that, then I knew that there was something that needed to be fixed.

I'm a little superstitious—if there's a task on a film that I think is quite impossible, and all of a sudden it works out, then I truly believe that the movie is going to be a great movie. That happened on **The Sea Inside**. There's a scene where Javier Bardem is daydreaming—he wakes up and he's actually able to walk, and he jumps out of the window of the house, crosses the valley, and gets to the beach. There were really no visual effects, but we made it work. We dollied

toward the window—the window was partly green screen. And then from there, we were cutting to a helicopter during the POV that would be moving and kind of flying down and then continue moving. Then that would seamlessly go to the actual remote headland on the beach. After we got it done, I told the director, "I don't think there's anything better that we can do—I think this is the take." And I knew then that the movie was going to be fantastic. There were several elements—not just the coordination of everybody, but also the wind and the remote headland—and actually making all the little pieces fit together in one take was very hard. It was quite a miracle.

I've worked with Javier Bardem several times,

01

and I feel we prepare for films in a similar way. Javier Bardem chooses films that will push him even further into experimentation than he's done so far. In the same way, I want to believe that I choose films that challenge me to create things that I have not done already. I want to choose films that will make me dream about that film that I might be making. I want to see the actual film I'll make when I'm done and be excited about it. It's easy: If the project is not engaging, if it's not exciting, if it's not turning you on, just let it go—because that doesn't better you as a craftsman or an artist.

When I learned that I had the chance to possibly shoot **The Road**, I was extremely nervous and I didn't stop being nervous until I was actually told that, yes, I was doing it. I really wanted to do it—I thought of it as being the biggest opportunity in my life as a cinematographer. I knew the book, and I read the script, and the script managed to capture the atmosphere that the book had created. But creating that atmosphere in the cinematography and being able to create that reality on screen was just the biggest, biggest challenge.

The Road was my first American film, but it was also the most European American film. John Hillcoat was a fantastic director and we were very close in our vision of how to create these environments. It seems like it might be simple visually, but the truth is that the post-apocalyptic world needed to feel real. I was

THE ROAD

(01–04) For **The Road**, creating a world that has been ravaged by nuclear war presented challenges to Aguirresarobe. "It seems like it might be simple visually," he says, "but the truth is that the post-apocalyptic world needed to feel real. I was trying to avoid days where the sun was out. I was not lighting much—I was trying to utilize as much natural light as possible. There was quite a manipulation of the process of the film to create a certain kind of monotonic tone for the color, so the work on the Digital Intermediate was quite lengthy."

"You control the technology. The technology doesn't drive what you do."

trying to avoid days where the sun was out. → I was not lighting much—I was trying to utilize as much natural light as possible. There was quite a manipulation of the process of the film to create a certain kind of monotonic tone for the color, so the work on the Digital Intermediate was quite a lengthy and thorough one. I felt that I was able to capture what the book was trying to portray, and I was happy about that. My only frustration was that the film was not commercially successful. I was disappointed, because I had given everything to make that film.

Right now is a crucial time of transition for filmmakers. And I have participated in the change, particularly recently working on the Twilight films and **Fright Night**. I got to experiment with all these different kinds of camera systems—Red, 3D—and I realized that while I'm very enthusiastic about these new systems, the craft of cinematography is more than that. The mystery remains the same, and it is a matter of adapting—there are certain variables that you do need to understand and take into account, but you control the technology. The technology doesn't drive what you do.

THE SEA INSIDE

(01–02) **The Sea Inside** draws much of its power from its naturalistic treatment of the true story of quadriplegic Ramón Sampedro. "Even though the film was quite sad and dramatic, I didn't feel I needed to push that with the lighting," Aguirresarobe says. "I was going for an everyday feel. I didn't want to separate my craft from what the story was trying to say." (02) Aguirresarobe with the director Alejandro Amenábar.

TALK TO HER

(01–03) Shooting **Talk to Her** allowed Aguirresarobe to work with the great Spanish writer–director Pedro Almodóvar. "The script was quite fantastic," Aguirresarobe says. "He likes his movies to be quite dramatic and rich in color." Because Almodóvar has such a defined style, "I would sometimes request his permission to change certain things. He was very generous—I was able to walk the fine line between pleasing him and keeping my own personal style."

Matthew Libatique

"Compositionally, proportionally and spatially, artists are doing crazy things. I think cinematography's going to have to stay in step somehow with street culture and street art and YouTube and the way people are making animated films, and incorporate them into live action."

Growing up in Queens but moving to California before he was a teenager, Matthew Libatique has emerged as one of the brightest stars of a new generation of cinematographers, shooting some of the boldest films of the last two decades. With his frequent collaborator, director Darren Aronofsky, he has lensed **Pi** (1998), **Requiem for a Dream** (2000), **The Fountain** (2006), and **Black Swan** (2010), expertly mixing genres to create wholly original, visionary and highly subjective portraits of individuals at war with the outside world.

Libatique can also cite several other fruitful partnerships in his young career. With director Joel Schumacher, he has made **Tigerland** (2000), **Phone Booth** (2002), and **The Number 23** (2007), lending a grittiness to the veteran filmmaker's post-blockbuster visual aesthetic. He has also had the opportunity to collaborate with one of his early heroes, Spike Lee, on **She Hate Me** (2004), **Inside Man** (2006), **Miracle at St. Anna** (2008), and **Passing Strange** (2009). Most recently, he teamed up with director Jon Favreau for **Iron Man** (2008), **Iron Man 2** (2010), and **Cowboys & Aliens** (2011). Libatique received his first Oscar nomination for **Black Swan**.

Matthew Libatique

" I was taught photography at a young age because my father was an amateur photographer and worked at a processing lab in New York. Photography was his passion, and he introduced me to it, but it wasn't something that I aspired to do until I realized I wasn't going to be a rock star or a baseball player. I actually played baseball—I attended Cal State Fullerton with the hopes of being a walk-on because I played in high school, but I couldn't hit a curveball. The one thing I knew as a child was I didn't want a regular job. So, filmmaking sort of made sense to me when I got into undergraduate school and was searching for what that occupation could be—that happened after I saw **Do the Right Thing** (1989).

I had seen films before, but **Do the Right Thing** just really struck me, and I started reading more about Spike Lee. I never really thought of filmmaking as something that was possible as a lower-middleclass kid with no exposure to making films, but then you had this guy who just breaks out and is more than just a filmmaker, but is sort of a pop-culture icon. At the time, you also had the Sub Pop movement: Nirvana and Mudhoney and Pearl Jam. And on the East Coast, you had Public Enemy and KRS-One—music was blowing up. Because of Spike and Jim Jarmusch and Richard Linklater and Robert Rodriguez, filmmaking was blowing up. It was just this explosion in pop culture that was happening—I got swept up in it.

I was hell-bent on taking film classes after seeing **Do the Right Thing**. I wanted to learn how to make films, but the only thing I really thought about doing was directing because I had no idea that the cinematographer's position existed. I remember making this short film, and I never really spoke to the actor except to tell him where to go for blocking. My producer said, "Uh, maybe you should consider cinematography." I was more concerned about laying dolly track and moving the camera than I was the performance, and I realized I was drawn to composition and lighting. So I started to pursue cinematography.

After undergraduate school, I applied to the cinematography program at the AFI. My reel

BLACK SWAN

(01–03) "The goal of **Black Swan** was to be as naturalistic as possible," Libatique says, "but obviously it's not a naturalistic story. Our aim was to place people into the world of a real person." Despite the story's fantastical elements, Libatique has always followed the same philosophy: "If I'm going to do something—whether it's shaking the camera or making a handheld shot—the application should be applied to the story. It has to fit."

"I was drawn to composition and lighting. So I started to pursue cinematography."

paled in comparison to most of the people that were at that school. I felt like I was in the lower third of the class—I actually remember freaking out one day where I just felt completely unworthy. But ultimately I had the wherewithal to connect with the people that I had things in common with and connect with the filmmakers that I felt told the kinds of stories in a fashion that I enjoyed. My first day I met Darren Aronofsky. I saw his work and I was blown away by it—it had everything that I enjoyed about current cinema. He showed a clip from a film he had done at Harvard called **Supermarket Sweep**—it just had a raw energy and emotion. I automatically responded to him.

I consider Darren my partner in my career—I really would love to make 20 films with the guy. You know, I think that early on we were very aggressive with our ideas and aggressive with what our intention was as filmmakers. That being said, when I revisit the first feature we made together, **Pi**, what I'm most proud of is the discipline and the subjectivity of the camera and where the camera placement is. There's a sort of a philosophy that we've had working together:

Develop a language that's consistent. The sooner you get the audience to buy into that language, the sooner they'll understand what you're saying. That way, whatever you put in front of the camera—whether it be reality or fantasy— it doesn't matter.

When I first started out, I was always drawn to the cinematographers that were loudest. I was drawn to Ernest Dickerson—I mean, when you look back at his filmography with Spike Lee, his use of color was very bold. Soon after, I started to research other cinematographer–director collaborations. I looked at Bertolucci–Storaro in **Last Tango in Paris** and **The Conformist**— Storaro's early work was just mind-blowing. And Robert Richardson was doing amazing work with Oliver Stone. So those three at the onset were huge, and if you think about them in comparison to other cinematographers, they're arguably three of the boldest ever to roll film through a camera.

Also, like them I enjoy being able to work with the same people again and again. Jon Favreau →

Recording everything

(01) "With **Requiem for a Dream**, I was obsessed with recording everything. I took Polaroids, I did diagrams, and I was very specific about color temperature. It was born out of a need to cement in my mind what I was doing. When I was at AFI, one of my instructors, John Alonso, was big on 'What do you mean you don't remember what you did?' Alonso would always get on our case if we talked about a film that we did and we wouldn't remember what stop we were at, or what the light was outside the window, or what diffusion we used. He was very adamant about us knowing those things. You don't want to keep searching—you need a foundation for what you want to do. You know you want a certain kind of light quality? Well, you should know how to get it before you get there on set. Every facet of the craft is about learning from experimentation, but if you don't remember what you did, it's pointless experimentation."

was having a conversation with somebody about my career, and he was saying, "If you notice, Matty's worked with directors more than once— it says something about him." To be honest, it hadn't dawned on me that I had. Along with working with Darren, I feel very fortunate that I have a similar collaboration with Spike Lee at this point—if Spike has a movie, I want to make it. I look back at a guy like Gordon Willis—he had Woody Allen, he had Francis Ford Coppola, he had Alan Pakula. Those are amazing collaborations. Part of the reason I enjoy working with somebody more than once is I have the opportunity to grow, and we as a partnership can grow.

When Jon Favreau and I worked together for the first time, it was on a $140 million movie. There's a lot of pressure there—it was my first

REQUIEM FOR A DREAM

Date 5/25/99   Int ☒   Ext ☐
Day ___:___   Night ___:___
Scene 126   CR#____

FILM EXPOSURE DATA
Film Stock 8572
Tungsten ☒   Daylight ☐
ASA on can   500
ASA on meter   1000   (comp)
DEVELOP
Push 1 stop(s) Pull ____ stop(s)
Flash % _____   Camera ☐ Lab ☐
FILTERS
Color Comp. _____ ND _____
Color_____
Diffusion _____
Grad _____
Other _____
Lens & T-Stop 29mm T 4
Shutter _____ FPS _____
Distance to Subject_____
Lens Height _____

Pola Stock____Lens____T__ Shutter I/____ Filter____

	LIGHT READINGS			TREATMENT		
A: Key T4.	inc. ____	ref. K____	gel____	dif.____
B: Fill T2	inc. ____	ref. K____	gel____	dif.____
C: Edge____	inc. ____	ref. K____	gel____	dif.____
D: BL T5.6	inc. ____	ref. K____	gel____	dif.____
E: BG____	inc. ____	ref. K____	gel____	dif.____
WDw____	inc. ____	ref. K____	gel____	dif.____
H: flo	inc. T22½	ref. K____	gel____	dif.____
I: ceiling	inc. T2	ref. K____	gel____	dif.____
J:____	inc. ____	ref. K____	gel____	dif.____
K:____	inc. ____	ref. K____	gel____	dif.____

Lighting Diagram

FilmCraft | Cinematography

IRON MAN

(01–02) Because of the demands of shooting a big-budget, summer comic-book movie, Libatique learned an unexpected lesson. "I used to want to come up with 'a system' to prep every film," he says. "Like, 'This is my method.' But that's idiocy. You can't prep every film the same way—I just have to go and do it. I learned that with **Iron Man**, because **Iron Man** was so different for me. I had been struggling with the method of prepping a film, and then finally with **Iron Man** I realized there is no method—there's no right way and wrong way to do this."

time at that level, and it was his first time at that level. When I first met him for **Iron Man**, I went into the office, and it's full of all this artwork: conceptual drawings, storyboards. I asked, "Where's the script?" No script, but there's a whole lot of artwork. That was difficult for me—in my collaboration with Darren, I've always been somebody who wanted to deconstruct the screenplay and figure out if the visual soul was gonna be derived out of the character or the structure of the script. With **Iron Man** that wasn't the case—there was no structure yet, and even though there was a character, there was nothing to latch on to in the way I was accustomed to working. But I knew the original story—it was a contrast between the world of these insurgents

and the world of Tony Stark—so basically that's the only thing I could invent in my head. Maybe it's just how I process what I'm doing, but I need something to sort of inspire me, so for that film it was about captivity, about that environment of the insurgents versus the environment of one of the richest men in the world. I just used that as a rough guideline for the film.

Whether a film is commercially successful doesn't bother me at all. I have no stake in the box office, and I never have really given a shit if the movie does well. I'm happy for **Black Swan**, I'm happy for **Iron Man**, I'm happy for **Inside Man**—I'm happy for those directors because it means something to them. But I could care less—there's no money that goes in my pocket →

Libatique's process

At the start of every film he shoots, Libatique draws a line diagram, like the ones here for **The Fountain** (01) and **Phone Booth** (02–03). "One of the goals for me beginning any film is the deconstruction of it," Libatique says about his process. "I briefly describe each scene in the script and do a line diagram in order. Then I color-code it—sometimes I do it based on day exterior/ night exterior, and other times I do it based on character arc." (For **The Fountain**, he color-coded the diagram to separate the film's three time periods.) "I'll put the line diagram up on a wall and take a look at it—it helps me clarify in my mind the flow of the film visually."

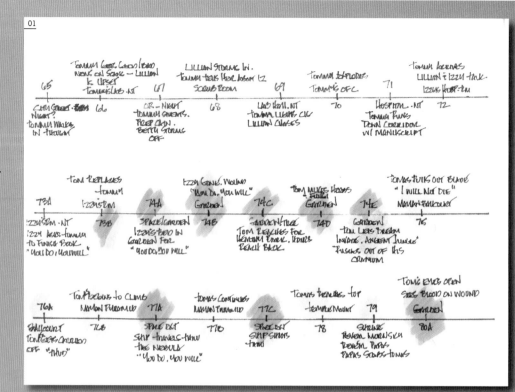

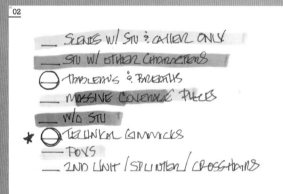

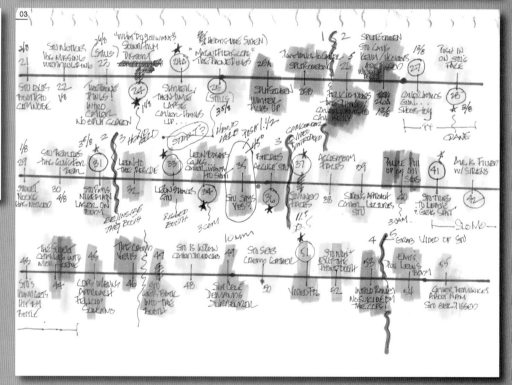

"I pretty much strive to make different kinds of films— trying to put a different spin on them and giving them what they deserve as screenplays."

directly from any of that. But I do care that people like it. I do care that film aficionados like it. I do actually care what critics think—you know, most critics, not all. And I do care what film students think—I care what aspiring filmmakers think. Still, it's funny: I remember the first time I had family members call me for one of my films and say, "I loved it," was on **Iron Man**. I think I'd made 15 films before I made **Iron Man**, and I never had a family member do that. So there's something to be said for commercial success.

I couldn't even begin to tell you what draws me to any given script. I think it's where you are at any given time, whether you're in the mood to do something with a lot of gymnastics: "Do I want to move the camera around a lot?" Or it might be: "Do I want something action-oriented, or do I want something more human?" Clearly, I think I'm drawn to drama more than comedy, but that's not to say I wouldn't do an intelligent comedy— one of the directors I'd love to work with is Wes Anderson. But there's no one genre or type of film that I'm drawn to necessarily. If it's intelligent, I'm interested.

I pretty much strive to make different kinds of films—trying to put a different spin on them and giving them what they deserve as screenplays— and not necessarily worry about servicing myself as a cinematographer. I'm sure there's a large population of people who look at the films that I've shot and find the similarity in style, but I work hard to not do the same thing over and over again—you want to look for something that's going to maybe help redefine what people think about you as a cinematographer. I mean, I look at **Black Swan**—I set out to make a very simple-looking film—and people still think it's bold.

I've made some turkeys. I made **The Number 23**. Terrible screenplay, and it's not a good film— it's an interesting film, and it could have been more interesting if the screenplay was better. But I loved making it because, creatively, there was a lot of freedom. We did some things in that film that I learned from, from a technical standpoint. So, I walk away from that experience saying, "You know what, maybe there's a technique there that I

can re-use." I always knew the screenplay wasn't good, but I did it because I wanted to work with Joel Schumacher again. To be honest—and if any cinematographer says anything different, I think they're lying—I wanted to stay in town. I wanted to be around my family, and I wanted to see my crew—that's why I took it.

When I'm preparing for a film, I'm always looking at photographs because photographs are very easy to sort of lodge in your memory and remember. I also look at paintings or revisit paintings that I'm a fan of, but there's also so much street art that's inspirational—maybe not necessarily from a cinematography standpoint in terms of lighting, but just concepts. Compositionally, proportionally, and spatially, artists are doing crazy things—I think cinematography's going to have to stay in step somehow with street culture and street art and YouTube and the way people are making animated films, and incorporate them into live action.

In terms of an actor's performance, I don't think we're essential like the director is. We have to put enough light on the actors' faces to see them, obviously, and the light is going to create a mood and accentuate the performance. But I think the bigger responsibility for me is taking the more macro view: How do I create an environment that the performer can work in so that they can find their character and feel comfortable to let it out? That's something that took time to learn. I like to leave the set open—I try to put minimal equipment on the floor so that the actors have something to see that seems natural. I mean, we go to the trouble of dressing these sets, not only so that we can see them in camera but so that the actor can feel that they're in an environment that makes sense for their character.

It also depends on the actor. Take Robert Downey Jr., for example. You take him into a living room, the first thing he's going to want to do is move around. I know that having worked with him several times—I know this guy's going to walk around. On take one, he moves around; on take two, he moves around less; by take five, →

"I've learned that the camera's not the cinematographer's tool—it's shared between the director and the cinematographer."

he's probably standing still. But that's his process, so you've got to give him space to be able to let the camera move around—it makes it more real for him to be able to move naturally.

When I was starting out, I thought a cinematographer was solely about the camera. But as I've grown, I've learned that the camera is not the cinematographer's tool—it's shared between the director and the cinematographer. We're called cameramen, but that instrument is a shared tool that we use in service of the script and the characters. The sooner you get to that point, the better cinematographer you're going to be. This is coming from a person who works with a lot of different directors he respects. If I was a guy who kept changing from director to director, I could see how I would think the camera was mine. But for me, I share it with every single director that I work with. Whether I work with them four times or this is my first time, I'm sharing it with them.

PI

(01) For **Pi**, an important early decision for Matthew Libatique and director Darren Aronofsky was creating the world of the movie through the perspective of its main character, Max Cohen, played by Sean Gullette. "We knew that Max was going to be in every scene and almost every shot of the film," says Libatique. "When he wasn't in the shot, it's POV, so we came up with a language of how we were going to shoot him—if we were going to shoot Max, he would be in closeup, but if we shot another character, we'd shoot over Max so that in every shot he was connected and the camera was as subjective as it could possibly be." The choice to use black and white was inspired in part by looking at black-and-white reversal films they loved, such as **Let's Get Lost**. "We opted for black and white because it gave us that sort of graphic-novel feel without having to have a lot of money," he recalls. "It's funny to think about the freedom we had at that point—making a small film like that and being able to shoot black and white because we could. Our goal was to be a midnight movie at Sundance." Libatique laughs. "It turned out to be a lot bigger than that."

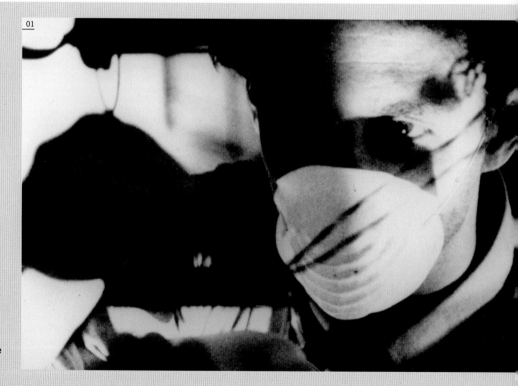

01

Using Regular 16

Creating the era: In **Tigerland**, the first of three movies Libatique made with director Joel Schumacher, the Vietnam-era, training-camp drama benefited greatly from its bracing immediacy. "We were looking at Frederick Wiseman documentaries when we were prepping," Libatique says. "Joel just fell in love with the idea of making the film look like it was shot in the '70s."

Making a brave choice with the stock: "We would just follow the action with a camera and then we would build upon that. We would end up doing multiple, multiple takes of a scene, but when you watched it over again on playback, the entire scene was in that shot." As the DP, Libatique's challenge was "figuring out how to place the camera in the time period and not apply the time period to the camera." Along those lines, he shot in 16mm, "but regular 16, not Super 16, which was a big problem for Fox at the time. They really didn't want to do that—they were wondering why the hell I was doing regular 16 instead of Super 16. And we were doing an optical blowup versus a Digital Intermediate. DIs didn't actually exist back then—it didn't come out until a year or two later. So we were doing an optical blowup off regular 16, which I pitched Joel on because we wanted more grain." For Libatique, **Tigerland** created an opportunity to make many such creative decisions.

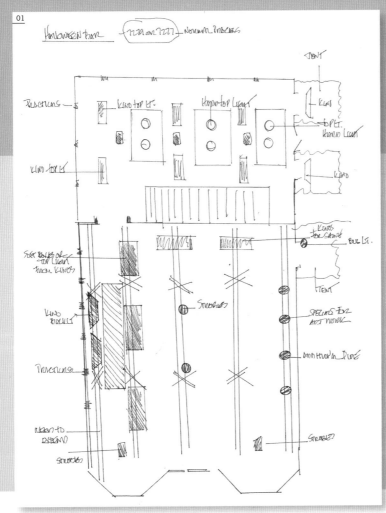

TIGERLAND

(01–02) For **Tigerland**, Libatique did extensive drawings to help map out the film's locations and lighting setups. "Film is a creative process, but there's time and money being spent the moment you walk onto a set," says Libatique. "The more you have an idea of what you want to do, so that you can get everybody moving in the correct direction, the more efficient you're going to be—and the more creative ultimately you're going to be because you're using your time wisely. Making a film is like jumping on a moving train. If you stop to take a breath in a moment of confusion, it's very difficult to catch up. You'll just get swept away into the frenzy of moving forward."

Freddie Young

With a career spanning over 80 years and over 130 films, it's not surprising that Freddie Young was considered one of the great filmcraft technicians of the twentieth century. He is best known for the brilliant spectacle of his color films with David Lean—**Lawrence of Arabia** (1962), **Doctor Zhivago** (1965), and **Ryan's Daughter** (1970)—for which he won an Oscar apiece. However, he was also one of the pioneers of the visual language of film in the UK in the 1930s and 1940s and invented the process of pre-exposing color film to mute the colors ("pre-fogging") for Sidney Lumet's **The Deadly Affair** in 1966.

He was born in 1902 and entered the film industry at the age of 15 in 1917 as a teaboy at Gaumont Studios in west London. He progressed up the ladder as laboratory assistant, camera assistant, focus puller, assistant film editor, then lighting cameraman. He had his first cinematography credit on **The Flag Lieutenant** in 1926 and in 1929 went under contract at MGM British Studios in Elstree under Herbert Wilcox. His credits in the 1930s included several films starring Anna Neagle, Wilcox's wife, including **Nell Gwynn** (1934), **Victoria the Great** (1937), **Limelight** (1937), and **Nurse Edith Cavell** (1939). He also shot the classic 1939 weepie **Goodbye, Mr. Chips**.

Throughout World War II and late 1940s, he shot some fine films of the period including Michael Powell's **49th Parallel** (1941), Gabriel Pascal's **Caesar and Cleopatra** (1945) for which he shot second unit desert work in Egypt, Anthony Asquith's **The Winslow Boy** (1948) and George Cukor's **Edward, My Son** (1949).

Shooting by now in color, he spent much of the 1950s in foreign climes on glorious lush epics for the Hollywood studios like **Ivanhoe** (1952), **Mogambo** (1953), **Knights of the Round Table** (1953), **Bhowani Junction** (1956), **The Inn of the Sixth Happiness** (1958) and **Solomon and Sheba** (1959). He even brought the paintings of Van Gogh to life, shooting for Vincente Minnelli in **Lust for Life** (1956).

Lawrence Of Arabia marked a turning point for Young. Although 60 when the film was produced, it teamed him with director David Lean for the first time and the partnership would prove historic. The scene when Omar Sharif emerges from a mirage in the desert lasted three minutes and was shot using a 482mm lens which Young brought with him from the US It is arguably one of the most celebrated sequences in the twentieth century. Shooting of the film lasted over a year in Jordan, Morocco and Spain and it was the first time Young had shot using a cumbersome Super Panavision 70mm camera, requiring ingenuity in the harshest locations.

Doctor Zhivago followed in 1965, providing Young with new challenges including shooting

01 With David Lean on the set of Ryan's Daughter

02 Doctor Zhivago

Russian winter landscapes in Spain with fake snow and the city of Moscow on a set outside Madrid. The production was again punishing—lasting ten months in Spain, Finland and Canada—but it afforded Young a variety of styles from vibrant colors to near monochrome. It was shot in real anamorphic Panavision 35mm, but blown up to 70mm for worldwide release.

Young's other credits included the James Bond film **You Only Live Twice** (1967), Franklin Schaffner's vast epic **Nicholas and Alexandra** (1971) and, of course, **Ryan's Daughter** with its stunning Irish sea storm. That was one of the last films to be shot in Super 65mm Panavision. The depth of detail and scale of composition that Young achieved in all these films has arguably never been replicated, and genuinely cannot be fully appreciated on a small screen.

Glossary

8mm, 16mm and 35mm Film formats in which the filmstrip is either 8, 16 or 35mm wide. 8mm is traditionally a home-movie format: there are standard 8mm and Super 8 formats, the difference being that Super 8 has a larger image area. 35mm is the standard film format today; 16mm is more economical and favored in television. Some films like **The Hurt Locker** are shot on Super 16 can be effectively blown up to 35mm through digital technology.

Anamorphic lens A lens used to created a widescreen image, today with an aspect ratio of 2.35:1 or 2.40:1

ASA A numerical designation of a film's sensitivity to light.

Aspect ratio The measurement of an image by width and height. For example, the standard 35mm aspect ratio is 1.37:1.

Backlight A process by which a shot's primary light comes from behind (or the back) of the foreground subject. This can create a moody silhouette effect on the subject.

Bleach bypass A process in which the bleaching stage is skipped in color processing with the effect that brightness and color saturation is reduced. It could be described as looking like a black-and-white image superimposed on a color image.

Blocking The process whereby the director determines where each actor will be throughout the course of a shot. This way, the cinematographer and camera operator will know where to place the camera and lighting to capture all the necessary actions, reactions and movement.

Bluescreen A special effects technique whereby actors or models are shot against a blue screen and then seamlessly imposed on a background. Green screens are more commonly used in film production today.

Camera tracks Like train tracks, they provide a smooth surface for the camera dolly to roll on during filming.

CGI Stands for computer-generated imagery, used to create fully digitally animated films or special effects work in live-action films.

Chiaroscuro A style of painting that emphasized a pronounced contrast between the light and dark areas of the canvas. This technique became popular in film noir, which made evocative use of shadows to create mood.

Closeup A shot that focuses on an actor's face or is close enough to an object that not much of the background or surrounding imagery can be seen.

Color gel Transparent colored sheets that are placed over lights to change the color temperature of a shot. Other gels can be used to change the amount or quality of light.

Color palette The specific range of colors that will be used on a movie. These are selected to create a certain mood or visual design for the film.

Color temperature A measurement of the color of the light in a shot or scene.

Coverage The process of shooting a particular scene from all the necessary angles so that there's enough flexibility to cut between different shots and have all the action covered.

Crane A device that lifts the camera off the ground, often allowing for sweeping or majestic shots.

Dailies The footage from the previous day's shooting, which allows the director and cinematographer to gauge performances, light, color and other concerns while the film is being shot.

Day for night A technique in which night scenes are shot during the day but made to look like night time. This trick is done by manipulating exposure and filters.

Digital A moviemaking technology that, like traditional film, captures an image. Unlike film emulsion, though, digital offers a more uniform image that lacks grain or the randomness of color and light.

Digital intermediate A technology that allows directors and cinematographers the ability to tweak a film's color in post-production. DIs can also help filmmakers blow up 16mm to 35mm with more fidelity than was previously possible.

Dolly A platform, often on a track, to which a camera is attached so that it can roll across a scene to film a moving shot.

Exterior A shot that takes place outside.

F-stop An adjustable iris diaphragm that controls how much light reaches the film.

F-stop A measurement on the camera to determine how wide the aperture is. If the F-stop is small, the depth of field will be smaller, because more of the image will be in focus. A higher F-stop creates more depth of field because less of the image is in focus.

Filters A device put on the camera lens to help shape how the light will be recorded on the film. Different filters can emphasize certain colors or affect the overall sharpness of the image.

Flags An opaque panel used to block light and create shadow, or hide lights in the scene.

Flashing film Exposing films to low intensity exposure to decrease contrast.

Floodlights A wide, semi-soft light source often used for general illumination.

Florescents A form of lighting that, rather than a filament, utilises mercury vapor. If not color-corrected, florescent gives off a greenish, sickly hue that can be good for creating atmosphere.

Focus-puller The member of the camera team who adjusts focus during a shot so that the correct person or object can be seen clearly at any one time.

Fog filters Filters that can imitate the effect of natural fog and lighten the dark areas, creating a soft, romantic glow.

The frame The portion of the scene that will be captured on film, as seen through the camera's viewfinder.

French New Wave A film movement that began in the late 1950s that emphasized experimentation with the conventional Hollywood storytelling style. Led by directors such as Jean-Luc Godard and François Truffaut, French filmmakers adopted untraditional editing techniques (such as the use of jump cuts) and handheld cameras for a more liberated and adventurous spirit. **Breathless** and **The 400 Blows** are considered landmarks of the movement.

Front projection A process of shooting performance against pre-shot background footage.

Gaffer The head electrician on a film shoot, reporting to the director of photography.

Gate The compartment on the camera where the film is exposed and the image captured.

Grading aka Timing *See* Timing

Grain Silver particles that remain on the film after processing to form an image. Usually, the faster the film, the coarser the grain, the less the definition.

Handheld camera A camera that is not bolted down to any device, such as a dolly or tripod, but is instead being held by the camera operator. This technique is often incorporated to create a looser, more real, more spontaneous and emotionally charged sensation in the viewer.

Hard Light Light from a small, direct point source that produces sharp shadows and strong highlights. The effect is more dramatic, stark and unflattering than soft light.

HMI Light A medium arc-length lamp which provides high light output more efficiently than incandescent lighting.

Interior A shot that occurs indoors.

Italian Neorealism A film movement that sprung up after World War II that emphasized stories about the poor, often featuring non-actors. These movies sought to capture reality as simply and directly as possible, focusing on location shooting and an almost documentary-like approach to filming their subjects. Vittorio De Sica's **Bicycle Thieves** is considered a landmark of the movement.

Key grip The individual responsible for overseeing all the moving parts on a film shoot, including the cameras, props, lights, and scenery.

Key light The light which determines the character of the lighting, usually from a natural source like the sun or a window.

Kino Flo A manufacturer of lighting equipment best known for its fluorescent tube lighting which can provide soft light and can fit into relatively small spaces.

Lens flare A phenomenon in which light hits the lens directly, causing circular colors of light to form on the image. It can be used as a stylistic technique, but is otherwise considered distracting.

Light meter A device used to measure the amount of light in front of the camera. This information allows the cinematographer to know what the correct camera exposure should be.

Location scouting The process of searching for locations that can serve as the backgrounds for the scenes.

Location shooting Filming that is done on actual existing locations, rather than from sets.

Long lens A lens with an angle of view narrower than that of the human eye.

Long shot see wide shot

Mark A spot on the floor where actors must stand so that they'll be in their proper place for framing purposes.

Mid-shots Or medium shots are shots taken from a medium distance, somewhere between a wide/long shot and a closeup. A mid-shot can show facial expression and body language, of a character, for example, but might not show the whole body.

Negative The strip of film where the image is captured before processing.

Noir A film genre emphasizing stylish lighting, moody shadows, and bleak worldviews. The typical noir is a mystery story involving a cynical private eye and a dangerous beauty whose intentions can't entirely be trusted. **The Maltese Falcon** is considered a landmark of the genre.

POV shot A technique of using the camera to simulate the viewpoint of one of the film's characters. In this kind of shot, audience members feel that they're seeing precisely what the character is seeing and experiencing the story through that character's eyes.

Practicals Lights that appear within the shot that are part of the environment of the scene.

Prime lenses Lenses which offer greater optical quality and have large aperture openings meaning they can be used in less light. Preferable, although more expensive than zoom lenses.

Rehearsal The process before the camera rolls where the actors practice how a scene will play out. Rehearsals can happen during pre-production as well as on set.

Rough cut A rough draft, if you will, of a film that allows the director to get a sense of the movie's overall flow before doing more tightening and trimming.

Saturation A film term meaning how intense (or saturated) colors are in the image.

Shot list A list of all the shots necessary for a particular scene or for an entire screenplay.

Soft Light Indirect, lower intensity lighting which produces soft shadows and less distinct detail.

Steadicam A device invented in 1973 that keeps a camera stationary while the camera operator moves quickly or over rough terrain during a take. The result is a shot that allows the camera to glide smoothly through a space.

Still camera A traditional camera that captures still images, as opposed to the motion picture cameras used for films.

Stop-motion An animation technique in which an inanimate three-dimensional figure is made to seem alive by capturing its slight movement one shot at a time. Taken together, the shots create the illusion of movement.

Storyboard A drawing that gives a blueprint for how an image (or a series of images) should look through the viewfinder. Directors and cinematographers will use storyboards to help illustrate their ideas before going on set to block a shot.

Take A recording of a shot that is captured on film (or digital).

Technicolor An innovative color-processing film company once renowned for its dye-transfer process.

T-stop A measurement of the light transmitted to the lens. Considered a more precise measurement than the F-stop, T-stops are used by professional cinematographers.

Timing aka Grading The process where the director of photography can adjust the print of the film to compensate for exposure and color variations. The process is known as timing in the US and grading in the UK.

Tungsten A form of incandescent lighting used on movie sets that is similar to the light given off by household light bulbs.

Tracking shot A moving camera shot that follows along with the characters through space.

2-perf Techniscope A low-budget Technicolor format which has two film perforations per frame instead of four. It was much cheaper than traditional film but inferior in image quality.

Video monitor & playback Used to judge performance and camera movement during shooting.

Video tap A standalone device that provides the same image as seen through the camera's viewfinder. This allows the director and cinematographer an opportunity to see how a shot is developing without operating the camera during that shot.

Viewfinder The device on a camera that allows the cinematographer or director to be able to see what the image being captured will look like.

Wide-angle lens A lens that projects a larger image circle than a standard lens, that can handle wider fields of view, create perspective distortion or enable large shift movements.

Widescreen An image with a higher width-to-height ratio greater than the standard 35mm ratio of 1.37:1.

Wide shot or long shot A shot that encompasses much of the background. The camera is at a distance from the actors, allowing the characters to be surrounded by their environment.

Zoom A camera movement in which the lens pushes (or zooms) in closer to what's being observed. This technique often draws attention to itself because it does not replicate the normal movement of the human eye.

Zoom lens A lens that maintains focus when the camera zooms in on the action.

Cameras mentioned:
Aaton camera
Optimo 14–290mm zoom
High-speed digital Phantom
Éclair Camera
Aaton/Penelope
Synchrosonic cameras
Alexa camera
VIPER camera by Thomson
Canon 5D MKII
Red camera

Picture Credits

The Art Archive/Contarelli Chapel S Luigi dei Francesi/Superstock: 86L; Museum voor Schone Kunsten Ghent/Dagli Orti: 37BL.

© 1993 Columbia Pictures Industries, Inc. All Rights Reserved. Courtesy of Columbia Pictures: 43.

Courtesy of Javier Aguirresarobe: 166, 168; Enrique Cerezo PC Himenoptero Mod Productions: 174T; Enrique Cerezo PC Producciones del Escorpion SL: 171BR; El Deseo P.C.: 175; Photograph by Teresa Isasi: 171BL, 171T, 174B.

Courtesy of Michael Ballhaus: 34B, 35R, 37TR, 37BC, 42BL, 42T, 42CL.

Courtesy of Dion Beebe: 103T, 103C, 107; Photograph by David James: 100.

Courtesy of The Blue Bone Production Dept.: 22.

Courtesy of Caleb Deschanel: 66, 70, 71B.

Courtesy of Christopher Doyle: 24, 26BL, 26T, 27T, 30B, 31.

The Kobal Collection: 44, 78, 90; 20th Century Fox: 19TL, 84BL, 84R, 154, 155, 120, 121BR, 121TL, 123T, 185B; 20th Century Fox/Page, Gene: 185B; American Zoetrope: 49; Anouchka/Orsay: 5, 77L; Antena 3 Films/Mediapro: 169; Artisan Pictures/Marshak, Bob: 52; Avenue Pictures/HBO/Coote, Clive: 165; Beijing New Picture/Elite Group: 25; Block 2 Pictures/Jet Tone: 26BC, 26BR; Cha Cha Cha: 65; Chaumiane/Film Studio: 76L; Chockstone Pictures: 172, 173; Cinematograph AB/Cinema 5: 145BL, 145TL; Columbia: 16T, 106, 116, 117, 187T; Columbia/Block 2/Jet Tone Films: 27C; Columbia TriStar: 148TL; Columbia TriStar/Gibson, Michael: 148R; Columbia TriStar/Wenk, Michael: 148BL; Cross Creek Pictures: 178, 179; Dreamworks/Paramount: 108; EMI/Columbia/Warners: 14; Enigma/Goldcrest: 96; FC Productions: 138; Film 4: 164; First Light Productions/Kingsgatefilms: 133; Focus Features: 56, 60; Focus Features/Bailey, Alex: 162, 163B; Focus Features/Chuen, Chan Kam: 58, 59; Focus Features/Kuras, Ellen: 140BR; Focus Features/Lee, David: 140BL; Focus Features/Sheldon, Jim: 64; Gravier Productions: 20T; Harvest/Truth & Soul: 184; Icon Productions/Marquis Films/Antonello, Phillipe: 75; Imagine/Universal/Reed, Eli: 62C, 62L; Intolerance Productions/US Playhouse Films: 136, 137BR, 137TR; ITV Global: 112, 113TC, 113BC, 113R, 145BR; ITV Global/Cannon, George: 113L; Jet Tone Productions: 27B; Killer Films: 51BL; Ladd Company/Warner Bros: 69, 144; Lucamar Productions: 102, 103B; Lucasfilm/20th Century Fox: 150, 151; Mars-Marianne/Maran: 81T; Marvel Enterprises: 181; Memorial: 92; MGM: 186L, 186R, 187BL, 187BR; Miramax: 104, 105; Miramax/Dimension Films/Tursi, Mario: 42C, 42BR, 42CR; Miramax/Dimension Films/Tweedie, Penny: 30TL, 30TR; New Line/Avery Pix/Sebastian, Lorey: 143BR, 143BL; Parallax: 130; Parallax/Chedlow, Paul: 124, 131; Paramount: 45R, 88B; Paramount Pictures/Duhamel, Francois: 161; Paramount/Miramax/Coote, Clive: 158; PEA: 81B; Recorded Picture Co/First Independent: 153; Reggane: 76R; Rome-Paris-Films: 76C; Rome-Paris/De Laurentiis/Beauregard: 77R; Screen Gems/Pathe/Bridges, James: 110, 111; Tango: 40T; The Weinstein Company: 98, 99; Touchstone/Foreman, Richard: 87B; Touchstone/Lee, David: 141; Touchstone/Sorel, Peter: 89; Trio/Albatros/WDR: 40B; TriStar: 68; United Artists: 21, 45L, 45TC, 45BC, 71TR, 71TL, 73, 122; United Artists/Morath, Inge: 139; Universal: 37TL, 95T, 109, 127L, 128; Universal/Marshak, Bob: 48; Universal/Olley, Jonathan: 127R; Universal/Tenner, Suzanne: 6, 29; Universal International Pictures: 63; Warner Bros: 15, 18R, 19BR, 32, 35L, 39T, 97C, 97T, 119T, 119C; Warner Bros/Cooper, Andrew: 38, 39B; Warner Bros/Appleby, David: 97B; Woodfall/Kestrel/Barnett, Michael: 93; Working Title/Film 4 International: 94, 95B; Yanco/Tao/Recorded Picture Co: 85BL, 85BR; Zoetrope/Columbia TriStar: 41; Zoetrope/United Artists: 83.

Courtesy of Ellen Kuras: 134, 137L, 140TR, 143CR, 143TR.

Courtesy of Ed Lachman: 46, 50, 51TL, 51TR, 51BR, 55.

Courtesy of Matthew Libatique: 180, 182, 185T.

© Ray Lewis: 176.

Courtesy of Rodrigo Prieto: 61, 62C.

Courtesy of Seamus McGarvey/Photograph by Linda Abbott: 156; Photograph by Liam Daniel: 159, 163T.

Courtesy of Owen Roizman/Photograph by Gemma La Mana: 123B; Photograph by Elliot Marks: 114; Photograph by Josh Weiner: 119BL, 119BR, 121BL, 121TR (3 images).

From the book Storaro: Writing with Light, Colors and the Elements, published in Italy by Aurea-Accademia Dell'Immagine-Electa. With Permission: 80, 82, 84TL, 85TL, 85TR, 86R, 87T, 88T.

Courtesy of Peter Suschitzky/Photograph by Liam Daniel: 2, 146, 152.

Courtesy of Harry Wiggins: 129.

Courtesy of Vilmos Zsigmond: 12, 16B, 18L, 19TR, 19BL, 20B.

Index